Rolling Waters

Rolling Waters

A Southern Memoir

For Peyton –
Beloved great-grandson
of Earl Riley Rich.

Love,
Aunt Phyl

PR Carpenter 9/2014

Phyllis Rich Carpenter

Library of Congress Control Number: 2014912915
ISBN: Hardcover   978-1-4990-5178-0
                 Softcover   978-1-4990-5179-7
                 eBook   978-1-4990-5180-3

Rev. date: 08/12/2014

To order additional copies of this book, contact:
Xlibris LLC
1-888-795-4274
www.Xlibris.com
Orders@Xlibris.com
638022

DEDICATION

For my sisters, Lynn and Judy;

For the awesome grandchildren and great-grandchildren of Earl Riley Rich;

For the O'Shields brothers: Robert, William, James, John, and Carl, who have become *our* brothers.

PROLOGUE

In the summer of 1957, my friend Linda and I learned to swim. We were both ten years old. I walked to the community pool in our little town of Smyrna, Georgia. Parents were not as cautious then. They didn't watch our every move. There was no need really. It was a much more innocent time.

Linda and I decided to have a race, starting off in the shallow end. Our strength lasted just long enough to get us into deep water, literally. We floundered, sank, resurfaced, grabbed for anything to hold on to, then sank again.

A teenage girl rescued me. The lifeguard pulled Linda from the water. We sat in the grass for a long time, never went back in the pool that day, and never spoke about it again. I certainly did not share the information with my parents. There was an unwritten rule in the '50s. You were not to cause your parents any concern. And my father was quick-tempered. Mother would say, "He can't help it. It's his red hair."

It was the most frightening thing I have ever experienced, before or since. My whole life, short as it was, did *not* pass before my eyes as I fought for my life. I had *one* thought as I fought to stay afloat:

Get out of the water!

By the fall of that year, I had managed to put the scary episode behind me. Preteens in 1957 were no different from those in any other era. We were just dying to grow up. I wanted to become "cool" like the teens in my cousin Danny's vast comic-book collection: Archie, Jughead, Veronica, and Betty. I celebrated my eleventh birthday on October 29, 1957. Just two more years to go!

Thanksgiving fell on Thursday, November 28, and was just like any other. Turkey and every fattening and delicious Southern dish ever thought of was served at the home of my maternal grandparents, Check and Francis Reed, at their middle-class home in the small Atlanta burb, Fair Oaks.

Not to be confused with *Gone with the Wind*'s "Twelve Oaks," Fair Oaks was a "community" named for its many mature native oak trees. It was not even an official town. Even today, it has less than nine thousand people and, except for actual residents, very few locals even know the two-square mile area exists.

Maybe the best cook in the South, Mama Reed turned out those dishes in a kitchen no larger than 8 x 8 feet. No microwave, no dishwasher, no double oven, no food processor. You don't miss what doesn't exist. Everything was chopped by hand, and preparations began days in advance.

A proper Southern Thanksgiving would include turnip greens served with my grandfather's homegrown hot peppers. With a perfect poker face, Check Reed delighted in watching first-time guests as the unsuspecting folks sampled his peppers, and then clutched their burning throats. He used me as a "prop" because I had been eating them since toddlerhood. And if a kid could eat them, how hot could they be? This folly was repeated often during my childhood.

No mashed potatoes or stuffed bird—those were strictly Yankee fare. Stuffing was called "dressing" and served in a pan. The only time you stuff something in the South is when you plan to hang it on a wall.

PHYLLIS RICH CARPENTER

We knew it was time to eat when Mama Reed told us girls, "Go tell Papa to glue his teeth in."

We ate in the separate dining room on the Duncan Phyfe dining room furniture. These grandparents had only two children, my mother Patricia and her sister Elizabeth, whom we called Aunt Betty. They were slightly better off than my dad's parents and possessed more modern conveniences, not that there were all that many to be had.

My father was telling my grandfather, Check Reed, about his planned duck-hunting trip the next morning with a workmate, Albert O'Shields. My grandfather knew young Albert because he, too, worked at Atlantic Steel Company in Atlanta. In fact, he helped my dad get the job when he came home from his World War II naval "adventure."

Twenty miles from our table in Fair Oaks, the O'Shields' family was sitting down together in their Atlanta house for their own Thanksgiving dinner. Claude and Ellen O'Shields had seven children, all boys except for one daughter in the middle. Albert, the oldest at twenty-five, had married a short time before, so the family meal included his young wife, Elaine. The two youngest O'Shields' boys, John and Carl, were exactly the same age as my sister Lynn and me, eleven and nine. Two sons—second-born Robert, twenty-two and fourth-born James, eighteen—were missing from this reunion. Robert was away in the Navy and James had just left for Army basic training.

Albert eagerly shared the news of his upcoming trip to hunt for ducks on the Etowah River, northwest of Atlanta. His father, Claude, was himself a hunter and had shared that love with all his sons.

There was scarcely a day in our lives that wasn't filled with some kind of excitement and I doted on it. Still do. So the day after Thanksgiving began with its own bit of drama. Before daylight, I was awakened by my dad making his way through our small bedroom in the dark.

We lived in the city limits of Smyrna, Georgia, now known as the hometown of actress Julia Roberts. It, too, is a suburb of Atlanta and just down the road from my birthplace of Marietta. Smyrna was growing quickly due to the jobs available at nearby Lockheed Aircraft and Dobbins Air Force Base.

Our neighbors' tract homes were very close to ours. So when our bird dog, Ole Jim, decided to bark in the wee hours of the morning at a night critter, a leaf falling, the wind blowing or who knows what, my dad was quick to get up to quiet the dog.

He had to go through the room I shared with my younger sister, Lynn, in order to reach a rear window of the playroom to yell at the dog. In the dark, he stepped on a toy on the floor and let out, "Damn it!"

Mother would have said, "He can't help it. He was in the Navy."

After he yelled at the dog, it immediately stopped barking. Not even an animal would disobey my father. When he walked back through our dark room, he said, "Girls, that room had better be cleaned up when I get home from hunting!"

1

Friday, November 29, 1957
The Hunt

First impression

Any serious hunter knows you have to get an early start. After all, one's prey doesn't sleep in. So shortly after Daddy's encounter with the barking bird dog, he loads the last of his gear for the day in the bottom of the aluminum boat, which he has secured to the bed of the truck. He covers the contents with a tarp.

Lynn and I were allowed to ride in the bed of his 1947 truck the first day he bought it. Never mind that it was ten years old. That just gave it character and value, to his way of thinking. The next day, the whole bed fell off into the road as Daddy was driving. My parents would thank their lucky stars it waited a day to fall apart. After that, Daddy hand-built a bed out of treated lumber. This new one would be safe.

The bed of the truck is missing side rails, a project he will get around to completing soon. After all, there's plenty of time. And if Daddy doesn't have a dozen projects lined up at any given time, something's wrong. He's a person with boundless energy. If he's awake, he's moving, planning, trading, buying, or selling.

His brand-new Browning A-5 semiautomatic shotgun is given a special perch in the cab of his truck. He had worked on a lot of motorcycles in his backyard garage in order to buy the $127.75 weapon, a fortune in 1957.

He then packs his lunch in the kitchen so quietly that my mother and baby sister are unaware of his movements. They are sleeping soundly. Just his usual canned Vienna sausages, bread, crackers, cheese, any leftovers lying around our small kitchen. He makes his black coffee and fills his thermos.

He cranks up the truck and moves slowly out of the driveway. The sun is just coming up. He's already smiling in anticipation of the kind of day he most enjoys, to be "one with nature." This day is perfect, one of those Southern perks. It was a day in late November without a cloud in the sky, the temperature more like a September day.

A light jacket would be all that was needed in the morning for the usual person. But of course, he is dressed like any proper duck hunter with camouflage pants, shirt, hunting boots, and jacket. And he had on his well-worn, camouflaged hunting hat.

He makes the drive directly east from our Smyrna house to the major road, Highway 41, leading from Atlanta north to Cartersville. He would meet Albert O'Shields at their prearranged point, a gas station on Highway 41. Before the advent of cell phones, *everything* had to be prearranged. Albert left his Atlanta apartment before daybreak, kissing his sleeping bride goodbye.

He is leaning up against his car waiting for his older friend, Earl, at their rendezvous point. His car is a new yellow Ford Fairlane—a fitting toy for a young man just starting out in this era following the end of World War II. He has a good-paying job at Atlantic Steel, a major Atlanta employer at the time, and a new wife. He has the world in his hands and was about to experience, as he imagines, a perfect day.

Earl hops out and the two shake hands. He asks Albert, "You ready for a duck supper?"

Albert laughs and says, "That sure as hell better be the case 'cause I was up at the crack of dawn on my day off!"

The two had been planning the outing for weeks. Since they were workmates, they had been waiting until their shift-work schedules coincided so that each had the same day off. They were grateful for the work in those postwar days, but alternating shifts of 7 a.m. to 3 p.m., 3 p.m. to 11 p.m., and 11 p.m. to 7 a.m. were murder on the body and family life.

Earl says, "Time's a wasting, kid. Just follow me."

He looks over at Albert's sporty yellow Ford and chuckles, "Try to keep up with this old truck!"

Albert is an accomplished sportsman in his own right, but this was his first time to make the hunt that was a regular event for Earl and his kinfolk.

The two-man caravan heads off for a perfectly innocent day of duck hunting, a ritual repeated thousands of times by hunters everywhere, every season.

2

In the 1950s, the world was still recovering from the Second World War and the country was full of young veterans home from that war. They were using their wartime experience to get jobs and buy homes.

The WWII veterans weren't just buying, selling, and building. They were making up for lost time. The Baby Boom was on! I was born within a year after my father, Earl Riley Rich, was discharged from the Navy. He had married my mother, a petite, auburn-haired, sixteen-year-old beauty, Patricia Ann Reed, in their hometown of Marietta, Georgia, in 1945. If my math is correct, I was conceived in Waukegan, Illinois, in early 1946—one of the last naval assignments my dad had before he was discharged.

The GI bill had enabled my parents to buy a little bungalow on barely one-fourth of an acre. Four small rooms and a bath, but it was a palace on its own estate to them. Daddy had already managed to add a small playroom and utility room onto the back of the house. He drew his "artist's rendition" of what the finished design would look like and sent off for some books on carpentry, plumbing and electricity. Just read the books and starting building.

He was turning the small plot of land into a "mini-farm" planting far too many fruit trees and vines for the space. Critters, too, like ducks, turkeys, and chickens roamed the small fenced area. If you went barefoot, which we all did, you'd certainly step carefully. The iconic ninety-nine-cent flip-flops had not yet burst onto the American scene.

Daddy had also built a small garage out of which he was following his life-long dream of opening a motorcycle shop. His plans were to have his dad join him in the business. He even wrote home about them during the war. But Papa Rich, my grandfather, would not live long enough to become a part of that dream.

There was always a steady stream of motorcycle enthusiasts in and out of our driveway and Daddy made extra money repairing or revamping these cycles. Sometimes they would come just to "talk motorcycles." We thought nothing of these comings and goings. It was just our way of life, perfect to my way of thinking.

By 1957, Earl Rich was thirty-five years old with a beautiful twenty-nine-year-old wife and three young daughters: my nine-year-old sister, Lynn, baby sister Judy, eight months old, and me, eleven years old by one month. His large extended family included his mother, three brothers, and seven sisters.

The day after our Thanksgiving feast was Friday and school was still out for the Thanksgiving holidays. My mother followed her strict Friday routine of cleaning the house from top to bottom before we set out to the store for the week's groceries.

Mother had been a "working woman" at nearby Lockheed Aircraft Company while Lynn and I were small, but she had quit work when baby Judy was born. She remained a very hard worker at home, and I can tell you the old saying, "So clean you could eat off the floors," was not just a figure of speech in her case.

We helped amuse the baby in the cart while mother shopped at the nearby A&P. The bag boys put the heavy brown bags into the car. Mother said, "Your dad should be home by now. He can bring in these groceries." She had made him promise to be home early from his hunting trip because we were expected at Uncle Jack's house for dinner that night. Uncle Jack was my dad's second youngest brother and was newly married, same as Albert O'Shields.

Rounding the corner, we could see that Daddy's truck was not in the driveway and mother was slightly annoyed. She took the baby into the house to change her diaper. I was small for my age, but I was one of those people born with the burden of wanting to please absolutely everyone. I thought my job was to make everybody happy.

I managed to bring in all the groceries without any of the brown bags bursting open or dropping any Coca-Cola bottles. I proudly entered Mother's bedroom where she was preparing to rinse out the diaper and declared, "See there. You don't need Daddy. I brought in the groceries."

The words were barely out of my mouth when I wanted desperately to take them back. I was immediately overcome with a horrible feeling. I looked down at the baby on the bed and she smiled at me with the same crooked grin my father had. I couldn't shake the horrible feeling, not that day nor for many days to come.

Earl Riley Rich was an ordinary, freckle-faced farm boy growing up in a poor Georgia farm family, second son in a family of four boys and seven girls. He quit high school before graduating, as many poor Southern boys did, to help his parents financially. Later, when he joined the Navy, he regularly sent money home to help with his young siblings. Like hundreds of thousands of young American men in the early 1940s, Earl Rich was eager to avenge the Japanese bombing at Pearl Harbor.

His brothers were Joseph Esco, Jack Douglas, and Harold Neal. His sisters were Edith Mae, Ruth Winnifred, Lola Elaine, Etta Athaleen, Dorothy Nell, and Ethel Winnona.

There were two odd redheads with blue eyes in the bunch, my dad and Ruth. The others had dark, curly hair and eyes so brown they were almost black. There was a spread of some twenty-eight years from my grandmother's first child to her last. In fact, her youngest child, Winnona, is so near in age to her grandchildren, including me, that for the longest time, I thought she was another one of my cousins.

My grandparents had named their children with unusual names. But what could we expect from a grandfather named "Homer Rosco Rich" and a grandmother named "Mary Ethel Iowa Jane Rogers?" Mama Rich inherited three of her names from an aunt, Mary Jane Killian and a great-aunt, Evy Iowa Marlow. Thank goodness they were just "Papa and Mama Rich" to us thirty-plus grandchildren.

I couldn't for the life of me figure out where she got the name "Esco" for my uncle. Until that handy-dandy invention called the Internet. It reveals that a UK company named "Mackay" has been manufacturing an "Esco nail" since 1912. Mama Rich must have seen the name on a box of nails out in the barn. Thus, Joseph Esco, born in 1916, was officially named after a nail. If you ever met him, you would know it was an appropriate name.

It was a miracle that Papa and Mama Rich's children lived to adulthood. Their antics are legendary now but mostly unknown to my grandparents at the time. Take the story of my Aunt Elaine. She suffered from back pain her whole life. She believes it is because she was the "tree tilter" in her childhood. If her brothers were cutting down a tree, she was assigned to climb it and *lean* in the direction that they wanted it to fall.

One such tree falling left her unconscious on the ground. Fearing reprisal from their parents, the other children dragged her into the barn and left her, not knowing if she was dead or alive. Elaine came in late for supper and the others sat in disbelief at the appearance of this "ghost." She got in trouble for coming in late, but never told on her siblings. Reprisal from a parent was the *real* fear of the day.

When I was little, people would ask my dad or mom if we were "rich," a poor joke about our last name—one we heard often. They would always reply, "In name only."

Well, my grandparents were rich, not only in name, but also in love and all other things that money can't buy. They taught their children well. All were honest, all were hard workers, and all knew the rules. For the most part, they followed those rules.

Aunt Dorothy would remember that when they asked for food to be passed, they had to say it like this:

Thank you for some butter beans.

Thank you for some turnip greens.

Thank you for some cornbread.

When my cousin, Leon, put together our family ancestry tree in recent years, he found a census relating to one of our female ancestors, Bethany Marlow. It said, "She was the most industrious woman of the community" of Bat Cave, Georgia.

So our energetic genes can be traced back at least to an 1840 census. Females in my family believe they can do anything a man can do. They fight against being left out of anything, no matter how unpleasant, difficult, or dangerous. I have been in awe of my seven aunts my entire life, even though their zest for life and independent spirits sometimes border on crazy.

In the family, there were two kinds of personalities. There were the ones who could talk on continually without prompting, like Uncle Esco. Then there were the quiet, slightly shy ones who will give you an answer or opinion only if you *pry it out of them*. Daddy was one of the quiet, reserved ones—except with close friends and family.

Nearly all my aunts and uncles could play a musical instrument. They never had lessons, just picked up instruments and played them. Daddy was the only one who didn't play. I think his shyness may have been the reason. He loved music nevertheless, and it was played in abundance from the front porch of Papa and Mama Rich's house.

Growing up with more than thirty "first" cousins, we just about played ourselves to death. I'm not sure we knew who belonged to what parent. We were interchangeable. We were more like brothers and sisters than cousins. I was perfectly willing to relinquish my sister Lynn over to another family. I'm sure she felt the same way about me.

Three of my dad's sisters also had daughters in 1946. The four of us—me, Vickie, Peggy, and Sandra—were inseparable. On these fabulous weekends at my grandparents' house, the cousins would chase each other around the house all day. I would stop circling the house occasionally to sit and listen to the music on the front porch from the banjos, guitars, and mandolins.

PHYLLIS RICH CARPENTER

Aunt Athaleen remembers Mama Rich playing the organ when they were little. Everyone would sing and Papa Rich had a deep voice. She said Esco always had guitars or "music boxes" as they called them, under the beds. There was no other place to put them.

The younger kids weren't allowed to touch them when Esco was away from home, but Athaleen would slip one out and try to play it. She was all about fun, to the point that there was always a sly twinkle in her eye. Mama Rich caught her playing Esco's guitar behind the bed. All Mama Rich said to her was, "You might as well come on out. I won't let Esco bother you."

Mama Rich was a tender and wonderful mother. My dad adored her and wrote home from the Navy in 1944:

"I'm okay, Mom. In fact, I've never felt better in my life except when you kissed me when I was asleep (you thought!). Remember?"

My dad began all these letters to his mother with "My Darling Mother." He concluded most of them with "Your Loving Son, Earl."

3

My father did not come home from duck hunting that night. My mother could not call Uncle Jack to explain our absence at dinner. He was just out of the Navy himself and he and his new bride did not have a phone. Phones were a luxury. Cell phones weren't even dreamed of yet. The thought of a phone you carried around with you that was not connected to wires and a pole would have sounded like something out of a *Flash Gordon* comic strip!

Mother fixed us something to eat and put the baby to bed. She was unusually quiet. I couldn't tell if she was worried or mad. But she did say, "I told him not to be late. Just wait 'til he gets home!"

Daddy had been known to get out into his beloved woods or on the water and lose track of time. Mother knew he couldn't help it. He was more "wild game" than man.

So the night before the hunt, she had a firm conversation with him. I distinctly overheard my father say, "Don't worry. I'll be home by early afternoon. I promise."

Eventually, Mother made us go to our room to bed. She shut our door, but the house was so small I could lie at the foot of my bed and listen to any conversation through the crack in the door. I drifted in and out of sleep, but at one point, I heard the phone ring. The call was from Elaine O'Shields, the wife of my dad's hunting partner for the day.

Dad had many friends but Mother had never met Albert O'Shields, or his wife. So here, very late at night, Mother answered the phone and there was a hysterical woman on the line, a complete stranger to her. Elaine had gone to great lengths to get our phone number.

Elaine Bullard O'Shields was nine years younger than my mother. She was literally screaming, "Albert has never ever been late before without calling me!"

Mother was trying to calm her, "I'm sure they just stopped for a few beers or had a flat tire. I'm going to send Earl's brother, Esco, to find them. I'll call you back as soon as I hear something."

I awakened again some hours later to the sound of a man's voice conversing with Mother in the kitchen. It was the middle of the night by then. I recognized the voice of Uncle Esco. He said, "I picked up Harold before I went up to the Etowah River. I knew exactly where Earl would put the boat in and where he would pull it out. Me and Earl have duck hunted together many times on that same river."

"When we got up there, both vehicles were there, O'Shields' car at the entrance, and Earl's truck at Milam Bridge, the exit point. Pat, it was pitch black, but me and Harold screamed up and down that river until we 'bout lost our voices. There was no answer—not a sound."

He had one hand in his pocket and one on his hip as he looked down at the floor, then said, "Pat, it doesn't look good. It sure doesn't look good."

My two uncles had stopped by the Bartow County Sheriff's Office on their way back into the town of Cartersville, Georgia. Harold said they had difficulty locating the office in the dead of night, and his patience was wearing thin. Sleep deprivation didn't help, either. So he said to Esco, "I have an idea. Let's screech up and down the main road and let the sheriff come to us!"

Uncle Esco could recall the happenings of that night perfectly even years later:

> When I went to look for Earl that night, Harold went with me. He lived right in front of the Spur station and there was a light on in his house. I stopped to get gas. I said to Harold, "Earl hasn't come back from duck hunting."

I asked Harold to ride up with me. Harold said, "Let's go get him!" I said, "One of the cars should be at the bridge. There it was!" I said, "There's Albert's car." The truck should have been parked at Milam Bridge where they would be getting out. I was hoping the truck would be gone.

Got down there, made the turn with our lights shining. There sat the truck. I got out and hollered for Earl. You could hear for miles. There was no answer. I told Harold, "Them boys are at the bottom of the river." He said, "Don't say that."

I had hoped they had gone somewhere in the truck. So I had a sinking feeling when I spotted the truck. It was all wrong. They would never have been out there on that water so late. They'd have gone on home before dark.

I stopped to alert the sheriff in Cartersville, Sheriff Frank Atwood, before I went back to tell your Mama. Frank Atwood said, "There ain't a thing we can do 'til daylight. At daylight I'll have a crew down there."

I said, "Well, I'll be back." I stopped by your grandfather's, Check Reed's, and your neighbor's house, old Mr. Harmon, and told them, too.

In her Atlanta apartment, when she thought they would be awake early Saturday morning, Elaine O'Shields called the house of Albert's parents. Claude O'Shields tried not to worry his wife or children, but thought enough of the report to call the Sheriff's office in Cartersville.

PHYLLIS RICH CARPENTER

The Search – Day 2
Saturday, November 30

After I heard Uncle Esco's words, "Pat, it doesn't look good," I drifted off to sleep. I told myself that it was all some bad dream or horrible mistake. Everything would be okay when I woke up in the morning.

The first thing I heard was the sound of lots of voices. There must have been a dozen people in the kitchen and cars parked everywhere out on our one-lane street. I felt a knot in my stomach, the same one from the night before. It would become my constant companion.

Mother, without explanation, sent us off for the day with a long-time family friend, Margarete Turner. Lynn didn't seem to suspect a thing, but I was already sick at heart. Normally I loved going to Margarete's house. It was large, beautifully decorated and she was another one of those fabulous Southern cooks. She baked the best pound cake I've ever tasted. She also made my mom's favorite, Japanese fruitcake. It was not heavy like the kind of American fruitcake we all know and hate. Still, I never made it past her heavenly pound cake.

Margarete was loving, pleasant and had the biggest laugh. But there was no laughing that day, just a gray pall hanging over my head, so low I could reach up and touch it. It was smothering me. And I was worried that Lynn was in some kind of dream world. It would have been impossible not to see what was going on, yet she seemed oblivious. As the oldest child, I had the automatic, built-in, protection trait for my sisters.

I tried to ease Lynn into reality so that she wouldn't be overcome when the facts hit her all at once. I gently asked, "Do you think it's strange all those people are at our house? And that Daddy didn't come home last night?"

She fired out an emphatic, "No!" She seemed mad at me for even asking. Was she in some kind of shock? Or did she really have no clue what was going on? On the other hand, maybe she was thinking, *"If you don't say scary things out loud, then they aren't real."*

Throughout the time that our father was missing, I would take her aside from time to time to try to help her digest some of the happenings as best I could, being a child myself.

Mother was dismayed that Lynn and I fought like cats and dogs about absolutely everything. But in all fairness, we two could not have been more different. Physically, I had my mother's darker hair, but with a blond streak down the middle. I also had her green eyes. Lynn had white-blond hair and dad's blue eyes. Yet, with just eighteen months separating our births, people would often ask my parents if we were twins. Lynn was a rough and tumble tomboy. I was a prissy, quiet, girlie-girl. We always shared a room. I was the neat freak, Felix Unger. Lynn was Oscar Madison.

My three uncles had been at the river since early that morning. And they would be there as long as it took to find their brother. Uncle Esco talked about going back up early on Saturday morning, after my mother's call to him on Friday night.

I got up a bunch of boats. Had 'em stacked up on the back of a pickup. I had just left the house and Jack was behind me, but I didn't know it. He was following me up 41 towards Cartersville. He'd see me on top of one hill, then another. He was going to try to catch me. He had a Ford. I went with him to buy it. It would run, but it wouldn't outrun that pickup—even with the boats stacked in the bed.

He never did gain on me. I went through Cartersville like a bullet. I thought something was funny 'cause I'd start to steer the truck and it seemed like it was off the ground. I needed sleep, too. I must have been running a hundred miles an hour. I wanted to get there fast.

It was just as warm as the dickens about 2:00 o'clock that morning when we first went up to look for Earl. You could sit out there and fish in your shirt sleeves. When I got back out there the next morning, near about daylight, the ground was so frozen it was

PHYLLIS RICH CARPENTER

spewed up high and I still had no coat on. I was just shaking, about to freeze to death.

And Check Reed walked up in a Navy pea coat Earl had given him and said, "Esco, put this coat on. You're as blue as a pair of overalls." So I put it on.

When Margarete brought us home early evening, the driveway was still filled with cars and others spilled over into the short street of just five houses. This couldn't be good. I knew it meant Daddy was still lost. One of our favorite people, Mickie Harmon, the daughter of old Oscar and Esther Harmon next door, hugged us and said, "Your mom will be home soon. And she will have a talk with you."

My father was lost and my baby sister was who knows where, so you would think I would be anxious for my mother to come home. But she could just take her time as far as I was concerned. I knew for sure I didn't want to hear the "talk."

I can't even imagine what the drive back to our house was like for her, trying to come up with the words she would say to Lynn and me. She was just twenty-nine years old with three young children, one just an infant. Her world revolved around my father, as it did for us.

When she arrived, I felt sick to my stomach. But I didn't want Lynn to see how upset I was. All the ladies in the kitchen watched us silently as she led us by the hand. Mother took us into her bedroom and closed the door. I had rarely ever seen my mother cry, nor was there any reason to cry in our perfect world. So when she was trying her best to hold back tears as she spoke to us, that alone was very upsetting.

Sitting on her bed, she held our hands as she said, "Daddy is lost, but lots of people are looking for him. We hope he's going to be found safe and sound."

She had to pause to regain some composure, "But if he isn't and it turns out bad, I promise you that I will do everything I can to keep things normal. Nothing will change for you."

Lynn and I would not accept that Daddy was anything but "lost" that night, nor for a long time afterward. We just wouldn't hear of him not coming home. Such a thing was impossible. We tried, even during The Talk, to console our mother and to convince her that everything would be all right.

"It's okay, Mother. They'll find him. He'll be home soon."

4

Friday, November 29, 1957
The Hunt

After about a forty-five minute drive up Hwy. 41 early on the morning of the hunt, Earl—with Albert following—arrived at Milam Bridge and left his truck. At day's end, they planned to boat downriver and pull the boat out, then drive back in the truck to pick up Albert's car.

They then drove together in Albert's car back to the Hwy. 113/61 bridge located just a few miles southwest of downtown Cartersville. Once there, they gathered their gear and carefully placed it in the little fourteen-foot boat which had been left at water's edge beneath the CSX railroad trestle.

This location was an excellent place to launch a boat and is still utilized by boaters and anglers today. At approximately 8:00 a.m., their duck-hunting trip was officially underway. They congratulated themselves on being on the water rather than back at the sweltering furnaces of Atlantic Steel.

Atlantic Steel's history dated back to 1901 when it was founded as the Atlanta Hoop Company, with 120 employees, and which produced cotton bale ties and barrel hoops. It became the Atlanta Steel Company, and then in December 1915, the Atlantic Steel Company. From 1908–1922, Thomas K. Glenn was the company's president. The plant's "deep-throated" steam whistle was named "Mr. Tom" after him.

By 1952, the plant had 2,100 employees and was producing not only hoops and ties, but also poultry and field fences, barbed wires, angles, round bars, channels, tees, handrails, reinforcing bars, nails, rivets, welding rods, shackles, and fence posts. The company was unionized, which meant employer and employees were subject to lengthy strikes.

Still, there was more of a "family tie" between employer and employee than what exists in today's world.

At the river, there was not a lot of initial conversation between the two hunters. They have all day to talk and it was still early. There will be many hours to converse as they sit and wait for *the ducks to find them*. The two men began paddling their way downstream in the dank morning mist, listening for flapping wings as they drifted in the steady current.

Neither man was overly religious, nor owned a suit and tie, one of the many things they had in common. My father was married in his naval uniform, and he borrowed a suit to wear to his own father's funeral. Albert looked out of place in a suit in his black and white wedding day snapshot, the only occasion that his brothers could remember seeing him wear one.

But any hunter can tell you that the out-of-doors is God's tabernacle, and a slow drift down a river is a religious experience unattainable in a building constructed of wood, brick, or stone. The sounds of the moving water and the wind in the trees produce a hallelujah chorus. The smell of the air, the plants, and the wildlife becomes the perfumed oil of Solomon's temple. Puts one right with God. No sermon necessary.

Around 9:00 a.m., they arrived at a small island in the middle of the river that has sometimes been called "the Shoals," "the Traps" or "the Brown Fish Traps" due to the site's location near the old Brown family farm. The island is part of a large, man-made fish trap, built by the Etowah Indians around AD 1200.

The shallow water surrounding the island forms a nice ford and it actually served as a crossing point for Yankee cavalry on May 23, 1864, during what my nephew Shane calls "the War of Northern Aggression," otherwise known as the War Between the States or the Civil War.

Union General William Tecumseh Sherman had surveyed the area around Cartersville before the war and had prophetically described the Etowah as, "The Rubicon of Georgia," his somewhat egotistical name for the river. Who knows what he meant? He may have had in mind Julius Caesar's crossing the river Rubico between Italy and Gaul in 49 BC, regarded as an act of war by the Roman Senate.

Sherman's army spent a full week exploring possible crossing spots along a five-mile stretch of the river. The fish traps proved valuable for impatient cavalry troops crossing the river in the wee hours of Sherman's advance on May 23. The local bridges were backed up with infantry regiments slowly making their way across.

One notable cavalryman that crossed the Etowah at the traps that morning was a twenty-four-year-old Irishman named Miles Keogh. Keogh had been recruited from his position as a cavalryman in the famed Vatican Guard in Rome to serve in the US Civil War. By 1864, he had risen to the rank of major and was an aide to General George Stoneman, commander of the cavalry wing of Sherman's invasion force.

Two months after crossing the Etowah, Keogh and Stoneman had their horses shot out from under them at the Battle of Sunshine Church, Georgia, during the famed "March to the Sea." After being surrounded, they became the highest-ranking Yankee officers captured during that 1864 offensive and Sherman himself had to barter for Keogh's release.

After the war, Keogh was assigned to the Seventh Cavalry under George Armstrong Custer to fight in the Indian Wars. He lost his life on June 25, 1876, on the Little Bighorn Battlefield. His body was one of the few that were not mutilated. This may have been due to the *Agnus Dei* medal that he wore around his neck. The Indians likely thought it to be some sort of "medicine charm" and felt it best not to chance repercussions. His horse, Comanche, was the lone military survivor of the battle having received numerous wounds from bullets and arrows before being nursed back to health to serve his last years as a regimental mascot.

Now in 1957, Earl and Albert would not have been aware of such fascinating history. Their interest was in the duck population known to fly up and down the river. And the grassy little island seemed to them to be good for duck hunting purposes because it is situated directly in the middle of the river. Ducks tend to fly up and down rivers and streams, so by positioning themselves on the island, the men would have been afforded rather easy "trap-like" shots instead of more difficult "skeet-like" shots from shore.

Trap shooting involves shooting aerial targets coming towards you or away from you. Skeet shooting requires shooting aerial targets flying from left to right or visa-versa. Earl spent four years in the Navy during World War II manning 20 mm cannons as an anti-aircraft gunner. The Navy spent a lot of time and money training him in the art of "wing shooting," so he was well aware of the increased odds of hitting a target when not having to "lead" it.

Arriving at The Traps, there was nothing left to do but to set up for the day's hunt. The island at Brown's Fish Traps is split into a one-third–to–two-thirds ratio by a narrow channel of water where Earl and Albert began to set up their blind on the larger, more comfortable section, though either section would have worked for this purpose.

They began constructing an "artificial" blind. To construct a "natural" blind would have required at least forty-five minutes of laborious rowing, brush collection, and back and forth trips. Earl was an avid hunter, through and through, and hunters understand the importance of stealth and efficiency. The men got in, set up, and were ready for action without wasting a minute of trigger time.

Having hunted the river before, Earl knew the game plan. The island was the only parcel of dry land on the river between where they put the boat in and where they had determined to get the boat out. There was nothing to preclude him and Albert from hunting from the shore along the way, but the island was their lone intended hunting spot. It met their needs for this particular morning. They settled in to their blind and began their patient wait for feathered targets.

It's not just about the hunting, as any hunter can vouch. It's the camaraderie. Two friends enjoying the open air and conversation. Albert is fascinated with Earl's new gun and Earl is happy to show it off. The Browning A-5 semiautomatic was billed as the "Aristocrat of Automatic

Shotguns." It also claimed to be able to fire shots off as fast as you could pull the trigger. It boasted of having a straight sighting plane, exclusive magazine cutoff, and shock absorber for comfortable shooting of any two and three-quarter-inch shell. This was a gun enthusiast's Rolls Royce!

And of course, the two will talk of their Navy experiences on this morning. Earl says, "You think this Browning A-5 is impressive? You should've seen the cannons I manned in the war!" He promises to bring pictures to work so that Albert can see them.

Albert has an impressive story to tell himself. He serviced jets on the ground at his two-week Navy training assignment in Corpus Christi, Texas. One day, the pilot offered him a ride. Being one of those people with a "need for speed," Albert was quick to say yes.

The "ride" was in a Beechcraft T-34 C Mentor, a light attack fighter jet used in training generations of aviators in the years following the close of World War II. This craft was 28.71 feet in length, 33.33 feet wide, and had a maximum speed of 322 mph. It could climb 1,480 feet per minute.

"Man, nothing's gonna' top that for me!" he says.

"Just wait'll you have kids!" Earl laughs. Ask anyone who knew Earl at the time and they will tell you he was quick to turn the conversation to his daughters. And he was known to brag a little.

Both men are situated comfortably into their "perches" for the day of hunting. Life is good.

5

Claude Albert O'Shields was named after his father Claude Elder O'Shields.

Albert's father married Ellen Matilda Caroline Hoy, a slight woman of Swedish descent, in New York City, her hometown. The two had met on a blind date when Claude was stationed there with the Coast Guard in the early 1930s.

Ellen then became one of the South's many Northern transplants. Southern gift shops are filled with cute sayings like, "I wasn't born in the South, but I got here as soon as I could." And, "No one ever retired and moved up north." The list goes on and on.

She loved the South but complained that people in the local stores made fun of her Brooklyn accent. Her sons assured her that the folks were just teasing her—that they wouldn't do that if they didn't like her.

Claude and Ellen had six sons and one lone daughter. The first two sons were Albert and Robert, then William and James before daughter Wilhemina. Finally, two more sons were born, John and Carl, in 1946 and 1948, just like my sister and me.

Albert doted on the two younger boys, playing ball with them and wrestling in the front yard with them whenever he visited after his marriage. As in the Rich household, the O'Shields household had its share of scary moments. Like the time William and James were saved from a stifling, suffocating death by big brother Albert.

There was an abandoned dairy next to the O'Shields' home. There were odd barns and sheds left behind. In a narrow alley in between two of those buildings was a fifty-five-gallon drum filled with hickory nuts. William and James were inside the drum cracking the nuts when they got to tussling.

The drum fell over, wedging perfectly between the two buildings, sealing the two brothers in what could have become a heated casket. Along comes Albert, who hears the faint screams of the two younger ones and rolls the barrel out. The two boys were gasping for air and covered in sweat.

In that case, Albert literally saved his brothers from death, but even the mere mention of his name came in handy for them. James says a group of bullies were picking on him and his brothers when James thinks to say, "Well, maybe I'll just tell my brother Albert about your threats!"

The bullies departed swiftly. Everybody knew what a strong boy Albert was, and that you didn't want to rile him.

Albert graduated from West Fulton High School in Atlanta in 1952 and was active in sports. A good friend, Ed Townsend, says, "He was elected manager of the basketball team in 1951, but he also played football. He was a fierce football player on the line. He had blond hair and sort of a boxer's face—pug-nosed—and he was a tough contender indeed."

"In those days," says Ed, "we could join the Navy at the age of seventeen as part of an entry program no longer used by today's Navy. It was called a 'kiddie cruise' and you could be discharged on your twenty-first birthday unless you re-enlisted, which I did."

So it was that Albert, while still in high school, quietly decided to join the Navy. His good pals from high school, Ed, Lonnie Quinn, and Gene Goodwin made the same decision, but were surprised to see Albert in their barracks when they arrived in Chamblee, Georgia. In unison, they said, "What are you doing here?"

Albert answered, "I was just about to ask you the same question."

By 1957, Albert was also into bodybuilding. He could lift three hundred pounds. So even though he was only 5'9", he was incredibly strong. Like Earl Rich, he could be described as quiet ('til you got to know him) but with a fierce temper. And he, too, had picked up some pretty strong language in the Navy.

Albert was not unacquainted with the Etowah River area. His father had taken his sons fishing there near the dam. On one occasion, the dam's whistle had blown to indicate a water release and Claude O'Shields had yelled at his boys to "get out of the water now!"

The brothers were astounded to see the power of the water released. Near the dam, in ten minutes, the water might rise twelve feet.

Second-born son, Robert, twenty-two, was stationed with the Navy in Texas when he got the call about Albert. He had been visiting his uncle who lived nearby his base in Orange, Texas, when the call came in from his mother.

Ellen O'Shield's voice was breaking when she said, "Robert, I have some news. Albert went hunting on Friday with a friend from work. They didn't come home. Your dad and William are up there now trying to find them. Robert, your dad is very worried."

Robert told his mother he would do his best to get home right away. He was struck by the fact that he had been unable to sleep the night before his mother's call. He had been plagued with the feeling that something was very wrong. His uncle took him back to his base where he knew the Red Cross and the Navy would help him with funds to get home.

At the same time, James, eighteen, the fourth-born son, had been in basic training at Ft. Gordon, Georgia, for two weeks. His commanding officer called him in and informed him that the Red Cross had called with an urgent message from home. "Your brother is missing."

"Which one?" James asked. He would be told when he called home that it was Albert. He was given a seven-day emergency leave home. A taxi arranged by the Red Cross took him to the bus station. James recalled crying the whole way home, with passengers eyeing him

PHYLLIS RICH CARPENTER

curiously. So it was that he was able to help in the search for his missing oldest brother.

William, twenty, was able to be by his father's side each day on the river because he had chosen to work instead of joining the military. As fate would have it, he had been unable to find steady work and was between jobs.

The O'Shields' home, like ours, was becoming overrun by friends, neighbors, and relatives—all who had come to support the family during the crisis. Although food contributions were arriving from the community, in time, Ellen O'Shields ran up a $500 tab at a nearby market to help with food for the many out-of-town relatives who had come to help in the search.

Normalcy, such as it was, had disappeared from the all-American Atlanta home of Claude and Ellen O'Shields.

6

Friday, November 29, 1957
The Hunt

About 10:30 a.m., fifteen-year-old Edward Shelton left his home and ventured down towards the river. Edward was enjoying a second day off from school due to the Thanksgiving holidays. He lived on Brown Farm, a large area on the area on the south bank of the Etowah, which had been in the Brown family since the late 1800s.

The Sheltons were cousins of the Browns and Edward actually lived a bit downstream towards Milam Bridge where Earl's truck was parked. Edward walked east along the train tracks that run parallel to the river until he got to the fish traps. There he noticed the two men situated in their blind on the grassy island down below.

Shelton did what most Georgia boys would do in that situation and called out to Earl and Albert, "Having any luck?" The reply was a definitive, "No," both parties having to yell to be heard over the rushing water and bustling trees.

Shelton then went on about his walk thinking little about the incident, but later reported to the Sheriff and reporters that, "One of the men had on a brown hunting jacket, and the other had on striped coveralls."

Shelton also said that one of the two men had what looked like "a pump rifle." In reality, it was a pump shotgun owned by Albert. According to police reports, Earl had "a new automatic rifle," information that must have been relayed to the police by one of Earl's brothers.

Shelton did not see a boat when he saw the two men but stated that, "It could have been tied at the bank, and I just could have missed seeing it." Standing on the elevated position of the railroad tracks,

Edward Shelton likely would have seen the boat if it were tied up on the opposite bank or on the island. If the boat was tied up on the shore nearest the railroad tracks, then he could not have seen it from his position up above.

His words make sense if you stand on the railroad tracks overlooking the fish traps. You cannot see anything directly *below* you due to a steep drop-off of some fifteen to twenty feet. Your view is obstructed by trees and brush, and you can only see the water at a distance some ten yards from the actual shoreline.

The island has a distinct and clearly man-made channel running through it. The Etowah Indians carved out the trough in order to form the focal point of their giant, funnel-shaped trap. As the Indians moved down stream shouting and beating the water, frightened fish had no choice but to be driven towards the rock formation, through the trough and into waiting nets on the other side.

Navigation over the V-shaped rock formation on either side of the trough is not possible because the rocks themselves pose significant obstacles on the south formation, and a combination of rocks and shallow water makes it impossible on the north formation.

The two men arrived with a boat, so it's there somewhere. It is likely tied up on the shoreline closest to the railroad tracks. Edward Shelton did not climb down the embankment to the water's edge below. He had no reason to climb down a steep, muddy embankment to shout out to two men, who by the way, could hear him just as clearly from the railroad tracks twenty feet above.

7

These are the touching words of the writer Norman Maclean:

> "Eventually, all things merge into one, and a river runs through
> it. The river was cut by the world's great flood and runs over rocks
> from the basement of time. On some of the rocks are timeless
> raindrops. Under the rocks are the words, and some of the words
> are theirs. I am haunted by waters."

My father, too, loved all waterways: oceans, rivers, lakes, or ponds.
He was one of those people who seemed more at home outside than
in. And my dad was making sure his girls would grow up with his
appreciation for all things out-of-doors.

The Etowah River forms Lake Allatoona and we spent every summer
on the lake, boating and fishing. The river itself, however, was new to
me when we held vigil there. Perhaps Daddy thought rivers were a little
too dangerous for small girls. That experience would have to wait until
we were older.

The Etowah River is a 164-mile-long waterway that rises northwest
of Dahlonega, Georgia, north of Atlanta. The US Board on Geographic
Names officially named the river the Etowah in 1897.

Some American rivers are named for fish, animal life, and
characteristics of the rivers themselves. But most often, their names
are derived from those given them by Native American Indian tribes.
Georgia's Etowah is one of those. Its name is the Cherokee version of the
original Muskogee Indian word *Etalwa*, which means "trail crossing."

It is the eighth longest river in Georgia. With its dam to form
Lake Allatoona, built for flood control and hydroelectric power, it is
important to Georgia and north Alabama's development and growth.

Georgians are not as familiar with the Etowah as they are the Chattahoochee—which is the longest river in Georgia at 436 miles. It cuts back and forth through the Atlanta area on its way to Florida and the Gulf of Mexico. Follow the 285-beltline highway around Atlanta and you will cross over the Chattahoochee a number of times.

This longer river, affectionately called "The Hooch" by Georgians, flows through Georgia and merges with the Flint River—then forms the Apalachicola River that flows into the Florida Panhandle. The Chattahoochee is one of the oldest and most stable river channels within the United States because it is essentially "locked" into place. It flows along the Brevard Fault Zone. It cannot meander and change course over time like most rivers.

In 2013, a sixty-four-year-old man named Robert Fuller completed a 1,503-mile river journey in his canoe, the *Sea Wind*. The trip took him down the Chattahoochee and Apalachicola rivers, along the Gulf of Mexico and back up the Mobile, Alabama and Etowah Rivers.

During this incredible five months, he lost thirty pounds and, just days from completing the trip, he faced the real possibility of drowning in a flooded river filled with logs and other debris.

Fuller, a professor, adventurer, scientist, Vietnam veteran and cancer survivor, documented the trip in a blog via his iPhone. In spite of the obstacles he faced, he said he would do it all over again and described it as "the trip of a lifetime."

View any map of U.S. river waterways and you will see tiny lines like capillaries stretching north to south, west to east. Some of these thread-like rivers form borders of states while others dissect states. The United States has over 250,000 rivers. The longest river is the Missouri River, a tributary of the Mississippi River, at 2,540 miles long. But the biggest in terms of water volume is the deeper Mississippi.

Healthy rivers are the lifeblood of our communities and are vital to our health, safety, and quality of life. They provide drinking water, with more than 60 percent of Americans' supply coming from rivers and streams. They also provide irrigation water, transportation, electrical power, drainage, and food.

Rivers also erode land and carry it downstream to the sea. This kind of erosion can even form canyons like the Grand Canyon and waterfalls like Niagara Falls.

The overall economic impact of rivers is estimated at $116 billion. And ecologically, they support a wide variety of wildlife and fish. The Etowah, for example, is home to the Etowah Darter, a fish that is listed on the Endangered Species List.

All Americans appreciate the recreational benefits of its river systems and Southerners are no exception. Rivers are often the center of community life and offer boating, fishing, swimming, hunting, and other happy events.

These rivers and the lakes they form belong to all of us. They beckon us to come out and play. But they are also treacherous and command our deepest respect.

PHYLLIS RICH CARPENTER

8

The Search – Day 3
Sunday, December 1

Two Duck Hunters Sought in Bartow
Cartersville

Bartow County Sheriff Frank Atwood posted a lookout Saturday for two duck hunters he said are missing during a hunt on the Etowah River between Cartersville and Rome.

The sheriff identified the men as Earl Rich, 35, of 106 Adams Drive, Smyrna and Albert O'Shields, 25, of Atlanta.

The men set out on a hunt about 10 a.m. Friday, parking their cars at separate points along the river.

Atwood said they apparently embarked on a 4-by-10-foot riverboat near the intersection of State Routes 61 and 113 near Cartersville.

Marietta Daily Journal

It might seem odd that our mother would allow us to be so up close and personal in the search for our father. But we were grateful to be included. Hard as it was to endure the sights, it was helping us to understand, one day at a time, the crisis our family was facing.

On this our first day to view the Etowah and the search site, our car arrived at Milam Bridge in the rain and freezing cold. I immediately spotted Daddy's truck. It was just waiting there for him to return. Later that day, someone would bring Daddy's truck home. It would be parked in the vacant lot across from our house where I could see it each day when I woke up.

I kept thinking that Daddy was going to be mad when he got back to its spot at the river and he has no ride home. This truck was his pride and joy. He would be upset if someone drove it without his permission.

At the river, Papa Reed, my maternal grandfather, got into the car with us, hugged us, and cried. He was always a very emotional man and known to imbibe a little. Well, a lot. He says to us, "I'll be your daddy now."

Preposterous! As if anyone on earth could take his place. Anyway, our daddy was only lost and would soon be found.

Then we went to sit in a car that held my paternal grandmother, Mama Rich. But the look of my grandmother this day alarmed me. Was this the same grandmother who didn't let us grandkids get away with anything?

She was a firm disciplinarian and most of the grandkids knew that. At any given time, there would be a pack of grandkids left with her at the old home place. This was daycare 1940s–50s style. Great fun, lots of love, and cousins galore to play with. There would be cold homemade biscuits, left over from breakfast. We would fill them with sugar and they were better than any store-bought cookie.

On one such day, Lynn and I were left in her care. I was not more than four, so Lynn was around three. Lynn crossed Mama Rich and she threatened to spank Lynn. So Lynn says, "You can't spank me. You're not my mama or daddy."

I had never seen Mama Rich move fast before, 'til she took off down the long dirt driveway in search of a hickory switch. Now she had large hips, having given birth twelve times (her first baby, a boy, had died at one month from pneumonia). Her movements were causing a local wake that made my hair stand out, same as if I were standing in a wind tunnel.

My cousins and I scattered like flies when the fly swat comes out. Some crawled under the front porch. The whole house, a cabin really, sat on little rock columns that rose about two feet up to the porch, so

PHYLLIS RICH CARPENTER

that small children were able to slide under easily. Me, I ran around to the back of the house. "The further the better," I said to myself.

Only my sister stood defiant on the dirt front yard. She was an ant daring a freight train. My cousins and I thought she was the gutsiest little kid we had ever seen. Or the craziest. To add to her bad day, Lynn received still another spanking when Daddy came to pick us up.

Now this powerful force of a grandmother sat before me looking tiny and fragile like one of those Faberge eggs. I wanted to reach out and comfort her, but I was afraid that just a touch or a word would cause her to break into a million tiny pieces.

She had bravely called each of her children not already involved in the earliest hours to tell them Earl was missing. When she reached Aunt Dorothy, Dorothy said, "Oh, Mom. He's gonna' be all right. You know Earl!" But Mama Rich said, "No, I don't think so."

A mother knows.

Papa Rich would be spared the agony of the search for a lost son. I was just three-and-a-half years old when I saw my grandfather die in our house. Everyone knew Papa Rich had heart problems, but maybe not the extent of them.

We lived in a little rented four-room house in Marietta near the downtown square. The date was February 26, 1950. Lynn was about 18 months old. Papa and Mama Rich and their two youngest, Harold and Winnona, eleven and seven years old respectively, had come to eat supper with us. Papa Rich said it was just about the best meal he ever tasted. My mother had made his favorites, oyster stew and shrimp.

Then we all went into the living room. TVs had been invented by then, but nobody had one that I know of. Papa Rich laughed his deep, hearty laugh all evening. I was playing on the floor. Lynn climbed on and off Papa Rich's lap.

She had just climbed down, when Papa Rich made a snoring sound and his head dropped onto the sofa backrest. My mother screamed, and then she and Daddy ran out of the house. I went over to Papa Rich and said, "Wake up, Papa." I wondered where my parents had gone.

Some years later, in 1994, my cousin Leon and I collaborated on a book, "Roots and Remembrances," containing our family tree. Leon's job was the genealogy. Mine was the gathering of memories of some of our aging aunts and uncles.

When I told my mother that I was writing about the death of Papa Rich, she said that I couldn't possibly remember anything about the night, because I would have been too young. When I told her where everyone had been sitting in the room and that I wondered where she and Daddy went, she couldn't believe it. Apparently, we had no telephone, and in the hysteria of the moment, they both ran to the neighbor's house to use the phone—leaving the rest of us behind with the dying grandfather.

Uncle Harold, just eleven at the time, remembers, "That day, we had fought a brush fire all day at home. It was just too much for him. Mama and me stayed right with Dad. Earl and Pat went to call for help."

So it will forever be one of my "flashbulb memories," one of those events so significant that we remember them forever. Like Kennedy's assassination, the Challenger explosion, or the terrorist attack on 9/11.

The 1950s newspaper obituary stated, "Homer R. Rich Dies Suddenly; Funeral Tuesday. Homer Roscoe Rich, a foreman at Blair Aluminum Company here, died suddenly at the home of his son Sunday evening. He was 54."

When Papa Rich died, it was one of the only times I remember seeing my dad sad. He adored his parents. My older cousins who remember Papa Rich say I missed a real treat, that he never said a whole lot but loved having his kids around.

PHYLLIS RICH CARPENTER

He was just as strict as Mama Rich when he needed to be. My mother told me the story of the time Uncle Esco came to the home place with wife Martha. Seems he had been drinking a little and said something disrespectful to his wife. Mother said Papa Rich went to Esco and said, "Son, let's go for a drive." Mother doesn't know where they went or what was said, just that Uncle Esco was completely sober when they returned.

Yet, he and Esco had the same sort of devilish personalities. Papa Rich would tell a joke but keep a perfectly straight face. It would take people a while to see that he was joking. We call it the Rich dry humor.

He also was a softie when it came to his kids. Once, Rheba fell out of a tree a broke her arm—with the bone sticking out of it. At the hospital, Mama Rich told her, "Don't holler, or Daddy will pass out." He couldn't stand for anything to happen to his kids.

The only other memory I have of my grandfather was of him lying in his casket down at the old home place where they lived. It was still the custom of old Southern folks to have their dead taken to the house. Relatives would *sit up with the dead* the whole night.

Aunt Elaine remembers from her childhood when she and my dad were given the assignment of sitting up with their Granny Rich. Evidently, Aunt Elaine and my dad didn't care much for her, nor did any of the siblings. Elaine tells this story, "Granny Rich raised something that looked like little watermelons, but they were called *quince*. She told us they were eggs. And if we took them out into the straw and sat on 'em, they'd hatch us out a horse. I now think she said this just to get us out of the house."

Elaine also said, "When we were told to sit up with Granny Rich, we were accompanied by our two cousins, Topp Anglin, and his sister, George. Her real name was Jesse, but everybody called her George. Instead of sitting up with Granny's body, the four of us kids went outside to sit in her buggy and laughed and cut up all night!"

9

The Search – Day 4
Monday, December 2

Two Hundred Seek Two hunters Lost in Bartow Area Cartersville

About 200 persons from four counties called off at dusk Sunday the second day of the search for two missing Atlanta area duck hunters who disappeared on the Etowah River Friday.

The search will resume Monday morning.

Joining in the daylong hunt Sunday were two National Guard planes, a civilian plane, rescue squads from Cobb and Gordon counties, a National Guard company from Rome and scores of civilian volunteers.

The only sign found thus far is a paddle used by the missing men, Earl Rich, 35, of 106 Adams Dr., Smyrna and Albert O'Shields, 25, of a Holly street address in Atlanta.

The three airplanes were unable to spot a boat reportedly seen several miles downstream from where Rich and O'Shields launched theirs on the Etowah at Ga. 113 and Ga. 61 near Cartersville.

The locks of Allatoona Dam were closed during the day to lower the water in the Etowah River that was almost spilling from its banks after recent heavy rains.

The search was ended at dark. Bartow County Sheriff Frank Atwood's office reported the river was too "rough, rocky and dangerous" for a night hunt.

Atlanta Constitution

Young Edward Shelton was not the only witness to the hunt that morning. Some train engineers also spotted the men. Their train passed by early that morning on a trestle that runs parallel to the spot on the river where my dad and his friend were hunting. Sheriff Atwood would get in touch with the train line and learn about what time the engineers went by on the morning of November 29. He would interview them, but Uncle Esco was not satisfied until he could speak with the engineers himself. His account of that interview is:

> Uncle Roy (Mama Rich's brother) and me went up to the railroad yard and talked to the guy on the train. The train was running double-header coming by there and saw them on the fish traps that morning. The fish traps were tore down on each end. The power company started generating and the water was coming up hitting them at about the hunting coattail. The engineer said he didn't see how they stood with the force of the water.
>
> The engineer said one boy had an automatic shotgun. The other had a pump. They even knowed what kind of clothes they had on. He must have been a hunter hisself to notice all that as the train was going by. He said the one in front was grinning up at us.
>
> I said, "That had to be Earl."
>
> The engineer said they acted like they knew what they was doing. "If they had just give me a signal that they needed help," he said, "I'd have tore the tracks up stopping that train. And we'd a got out and helped them."
>
> I said, "Maybe they didn't figure they needed any help."

Mother, thinking Daddy will be found any minute now, has allowed Lynn and me to stay home from school. We would be out for the whole week, but still no word about my dad. Lynn and I were intrigued by the search and were grateful to be included, rather than being treated like children. Both of us were absolutely sure he was just "lost" and would come out of the woods at any moment. A search of the *water* was a waste of time, as far as we were concerned.

I overheard my cousin Leon, a teenager by 1957, expressing the same reservations about the search. How could his uncle, larger than life, let a little thing like a river get the best of him? He said, "Earl gave me my first gun, which I still have. It had such a kick to it that the first time I used it, it busted my nose and mouth. I'm thinking that's why he gave it to me."

"Me and Jack, Harold and Tommy followed Earl and Esco around everywhere, trying to keep up with them. On one of those trips, Earl got bitten by a squirrel. He had shot it and it ran up a tree. When he put his hand up in the tree to get it, it bit the heck out of him. Earl just wrapped it up with a handkerchief."

"And then there was the time," Leon went on to say, "when Esco, Earl, Harold and Jack went fishing up on Little River. They got in a Johnboat and it sunk so deep, the water was way up nearly over the edge of the boat. They seriously wanted me to get in! But I refused."

"They were real daring. If Earl and Esco were in a boat out on Papa Rich's lake, there'd be a turtle come up and they'd shoot it in the head with a .22 rifle and just dive right over in the water to go after it."

One day while standing at the riverbank, something caught Lynn's eye in the trees on the other side. It looked to her like a man's form and he appeared to be wearing our dad's hunting cap. She ran to tell Aunt Athaleen and Aunt Dorothy, but they didn't see anything in the woods. Lynn thought Daddy might need help so she persisted. Our aunts took her by the hand and walked her across Milam Bridge to the other side.

National Guardsmen were posted at both ends of the bridge because only guardsmen, searchers, and family members were allowed across the bridge. That was a security measure to keep the throngs of sightseers from interfering with the search. As Lynn and our aunts approached the soldier on the far side and explained the situation to him, he immediately walked to the edge of the trees and began cutting a path as Lynn pointed the way.

After a few minutes, he reached the spot where she thought she saw our father, but there was no one there. She walked slowly back to the camp with our aunts. She was very quiet the rest of the day.

At the same time all this commotion was going on, witnesses, including William O'Shields, Albert's twenty-year-old brother, were standing on the bridge taking in the scene. A small crowd was gathering. Rumors ran rampant in those days of no cell phones.

Back at one of the National Guard tents that evening, where William and his father Claude were spending the night, the guardsmen were asking what was going on up at Milam Bridge that morning. The commander said quietly, "The little girl thought she saw her daddy in the woods."

William said all heads looked down and no one spoke about it after that. In 1957, we were totally oblivious to the pain even the searchers were experiencing. But it seems that every one of them wanted to bring the nightmare to a close, most preferably with a happy ending. Many of the searchers had young children themselves.

Why exactly did Lynn think Daddy would hide from us in the woods? I might have been the only one to understand the deeper meaning. We had often been on hunting and fishing trips with our dad. He would use those occasions to teach us the "lessons of the wild." On one such trip to hunt squirrels, he woke us early one Saturday morning. Mother was expecting Judy and not feeling well, so he was probably giving her a day's break from us.

He instructed us to dress in such a way that we would blend in with the woods. That way, the animals would not see us. Okay, so we looked through our stash of pastel, girly clothes and came up with the woodsiest outfits we could find, but I'm quite sure that no critters were fooled by us that day.

Later, we were deep in the woods in the middle of nowhere. Daddy was shooting the squirrels and we were putting them into the little baskets he had given each of us. Then he says, "I'm going on up ahead and when I call you, come meet me."

Alone, we felt like Little Red Riding Hood, one-step away from a wolf's lunch—us being the lunch. Finally, I heard Dad call from way off and we headed to the sound of his voice. Once we got there, he was nowhere in sight.

We were quietly discussing what to do in lieu of our grave circumstances when I spotted The Grin, not ten feet away from us. He had been that close but blended completely into the surroundings. If he hadn't grinned, we'd have never seen him. Before we discovered him, I'm sure he enjoyed our conversation as we discussed Plan B for getting ourselves *unlost*.

That same day, he took us to a little general store somewhere in North Georgia for drinks and food. Behind the counter was a bona fide *giant*. The man must have been over seven feet tall, with the frame and girth to go with his height. Lynn and I looked up with our mouths wide open. We could barely talk.

It was clear that Daddy knew this man and they seemed happy to see each other. Daddy asked him how his little girls were doing. I was shocked. Who would marry a scary giant?

When we got in the car, Daddy told us we would never meet a better man than the one in the store. And that we should never ever judge a man by his outward appearance or by the things he possesses—only by the person he was inside. It is a lesson I have never forgotten.

Now, about squirrels! They were a staple in the poor Southerner's diet when we were children, along with anything else that could be caught or shot. They were delicious fried for breakfast, to go with biscuits and gravy. I was exposed to very little store-bought meat when I was a child.

Rabbits, too! Both were considered a patriotic food during World War II, but went out of fashion later. Rabbits "are helping win the war," proclaimed a *Los Angeles Times* article from 1943. Thousands of Americans raised them in their backyards. Along with victory gardens, rabbits and other wild game helped put food on the table when much of the nations' supply was shipped to soldiers overseas and ration stamps provided little at home.

Rabbit appears to be going through a renaissance in our modern world. But squirrels? Well, they've never really caught back on. Today, I buy feed for the squirrels in my backyard. Well, actually, I buy the food for the deer. The squirrels just help themselves. Their species doesn't seem to have suffered much from their decades of being served up for Southern breakfasts.

During those years, firearms were a necessity, not a vanity thing. If you were poor and didn't have a gun, you could starve. They were used with caution and respect. Daddy's guns were always kept locked in a gun cabinet. After each use, he cleaned them like they were worth a fortune.

10

Friday, November 29, 1957
The Hunt

This trip was not rocket science and there was no meticulous plan in place. The two men were on an adventure with guns, and there's not a "good ole' boy" worth his salt that would not have gladly signed up at the drop of a hat to join them that day, plan or no plan.

But the location of the boat during Earl and Albert's time on the island is critical to this story. From a hunting perspective, the logical place to position a boat in order to retrieve downed ducks would be in the trough itself! If the boat is anchored in the trough and a duck is shot, then one of the men simply hops into the boat and makes a quick retrieval downstream or on either side of the island.

Earl sometimes used his boat as part of a blind. Even today, you see examples of boats being made into "floating blinds," with artificial grass and reeds incorporated onto the sides and top of them. But the men were not floating *in* the water that day. If they had been, any rising water issue would not have created a crisis.

They were actually sitting *on* the island. If the boat had been with them, then its lower section would have been clearly visible to Edward Shelton. Considering that Shelton's description of the men was remarkably detail-oriented, one would have to believe that even a boat that was sporting today's high-tech camouflage designs would have been easy for him to visually spot. Hand-painted camouflage patterns from the 1950s were not exactly "lifelike." Besides, if the men utilized the boat itself as part of the blind, then they would have to disassemble the blind every time they had to launch the boat to retrieve a dead duck.

Having the boat with them on the island would have been the logical thing to do, but they were there to hunt ducks. The boat would be something the ducks would easily pick out from above.

There is much debate as to how smart ducks are, but there is agreement that their communication skills are excellent. Mess with one of them, and all heck breaks loose, with the others honking and hissing. Seasoned hunters wouldn't go to the trouble of trying to hide from them if they hadn't learned over time that it's necessary.

The water was up considerably from recent rains, but the men were in the field hunting and were probably ready to roll with whatever situation they encountered, within reason. Getting their boots and socks wet might not have been that big of a deal to them.

One would think that if they shot a duck downstream from the island, recovery would be next to impossible. Their setup was awkward from a practical standpoint, but the only explanation is that the two men accepted the fact that if they shot a duck, one of them would have to traverse the rocks on either side of the island to intercept it as it floated downstream.

If they had shot a duck downstream from the island (with or without the boat), recovery of the bird would have been next to impossible as it quickly floated away. Even if they managed to catch up with the bird, they would have to make their way back upstream to the island, against the current.

Another inconvenient fact is that they did not have a dog with them to retrieve birds. Ole Jim was a "land" dog. There's no telling where he'd wind up if you put him in a boat.

Therefore, the boat being placed on the south shoreline a short distance from the island actually makes sense. While probably a simple decision to them that morning, it would prove to be a problematic one.

About the time Edward Shelton was calling out to Earl and Albert by the river, engineers at the Allatoona Dam set off a warning siren and then started up both of the dam's generators to begin releasing water in response to electric demands in the area.

There are two ways water is released at the dam:

1) Power turbines release water at the bottom of the dam for generating electricity. This process is called "sluicing".

2) When rains have been heavy, spill gates alleviate pressure by releasing water through spill gates over the top of the dam.

These spills are controlled. They do not take place spontaneously. They may amount to a one-inch or two-inch release, or up to a three-foot release. They will cause a gradual rise in depth of water downstream. It may have taken thirty minutes to one hour to reach the location of the hunters. The real danger to anyone recreating in the area would probably have been water current and temperature—not depth.

According to the historical data of the U.S. Geologic Survey, the release was of a normal range that day with nothing to indicate that trouble would occur downstream.

Hunters in today's world can call a phone number and receive a recorded "generation schedule." What means were available to the hunters in 1957 is unclear. What is known is that locals, including Earl and Albert, would have been aware of the possibility of generating waters.

A freight train happened to pass by minutes after the rising water had reached the traps. The engineers were surprised to see two men in the water below. The engineers must have been locals who were familiar with that particular route because they specifically referred to the spot as the "old Indian fish traps." They reported Earl and Albert to have been in "waist deep water," attempting to traverse the south rock formation with their guns above their heads and *no boat in sight*.

They had such a clear view of the men, that one engineer noted a "grin" on Earl's face as he looked up at the passing train. Perhaps

Earl appreciated the awkwardness of that moment from the engineer's perspective more than he did the growing danger of his own.

Due to sight-line restrictions from the tracks above (and this is important) the two men had to have been at least ten yards from the bank for the engineers to have been able to physically see them at all.

11

The Search - Day 5
Tuesday, December 3

Two Men Still Missing on Etowah River
Search Enters Another Day Today With No Trace of Duck Hunters

Dragging of the Etowah River was continued today, as searchers sought the bodies of two men, missing since Friday, or evidence leading to their whereabouts.

Missing are Earl Rich, 35, of Smyrna and Albert O'Shields, 25, of Atlanta.

Better than 200 persons joined in the search Sunday for the two men who were probably last seen about 10:30 a.m. Friday morning.

Taking part in the search were members of the Bartow Sheriff's Office, the Cartersville Police Department, GBI Agents, members of the 163rd Tank Battalion, two National Guard planes, civilian planes and Civil Defense Reserve squads from Calhoun and Smyrna, as well as the local Civil Defense unit.

The search was begun Saturday morning when relatives of Rich came to Cartersville hunting the two men who had not returned home Friday night as expected.

Sheriff Atwood was contacted and the area was canvassed for the two men and people questioned about having seen them.

Through Monday morning, the only trace of the two men were the car and truck they had left and one paddle, found floating on the river near the Milam Bridge at Euharlee.

The two men were seen around 10:30 a.m. Friday going into the river at the bridge on State Highway 61 near Ladds.

They had left a small truck at the Milam Bridge and returned by car to the bridge at Ladds where they left that car, presumably intending to go by boat downstream to where they had left their truck.

Fifteen-year-old Edward Shelton who resides on the Brown Farm reporting seeing two men on the rock "fish trap" located between the Brown Farm on the south bank and the Stiles Farm on the north bank of the river.

He said the two were behind a blind of brush piled by duck hunters to get on the shoals. He called to the two men asking if they were having any luck. The youth said they answered, "No," and he left thinking little of the incident.

Shelton told a Tribune News reporter that one of the men had on a brown hunting jacket and the other had on striped coveralls. He said one of the two men had what looked like, at a distance, a pump rifle.

According to police, both men were wearing hunting jackets and at least one of the men was wearing coveralls. Rich had a new automatic rifle.

The youth said he did not see a boat but said that it could have been tied at the bank out of his eyesight.

As of noon Monday, there has been no trace of the men, their boat (with the exception of the paddle), or any of their clothing or personal belongings that might give a hint as to what has happened to them.

Members of the families of both men were at the scene most all day Sunday. Rich was married and the father of three children. O'Shields had been married less than a year. Both men had worked at the Atlantic Steel firm.

The Daily Tribune News
Cartersville, Georgia

Back home from the search that night, my teacher called and asked to speak to me. Now, no fourth-grader wants to get a phone call at home from her teacher. School, which I had always loved, now seemed a million years behind me.

This particular teacher had a reputation for being strict and no-nonsense. Now her voice was so sweet, I barely recognized her as she said, "Phyllis, your classmates and I are missing you each day at school. We all hope your dad will be found safe and sound, and that you will return real soon."

I have no idea what I said in return.

The Search - Day 6
Wednesday, December 4

Empty Boat Gives Clue for Search
Craft Believed Used By Hunters Missing 4 Days
Still No Trace of Pair Missing on Etowah River

An empty boat believed used by two duck hunters who have been missing on the Etowah River since Friday was spotted by a helicopter around noon on Monday.

A helicopter brought into the search for the first time yesterday observed the boat at a point 10 miles from Milam Bridge, where the two hunters reportedly entered the water.

Some 200 searchers had confined their hunt to a four-mile area from the bridge, believing the boat could not have drifted further. Discovery of the boat was made at the Thompson Wiseman Farm, near the Floyd-Bartow line.

Searchers quit at dusk Sunday after covering the area where Earl Rich and Albert O'Shields were last seen. A paddle from their boat had been the only clue turned up.

The Smyrna Fire Department rescue unit was sent to the scene Monday and Cobb County policemen and Sheriff's deputies joined in the hunt.

Since Governor Marvin Griffin gave authorization Saturday, the Rome Unit of the Georgia National Guard has participated in the search, along with the Civil Air Patrol, rescue squads, and volunteers.

PHYLLIS RICH CARPENTER

The men launched their boat on the Etowah near Cartersville Friday.
The river was almost out of its banks from heavy rains and Sunday
the locks of Allatoona dam were kept closed to lower the water level.

Marietta Daily Journal

Esco reported: The Hughes' boys had a airplane they used to look for Earl overhead. They had done found a boat down river. They was looking for me that evening. Wanted me to ride in the airplane with them to see if that was the boat.

When we identified it, the National Guard flew over the spot with their helicopter. Then they took some equipment down there to get it out. But it was hung up in the brush and it was so late, the sky was getting dark. They couldn't get it out.

My sisters said, "We'll go get it." They talked one guardsman into taking them down to the spot in one of the government trucks, but the guard said it was "too muddy" to get to the area.

My sisters ignored him, went down there, tore it loose, and got it out. You should have seen the embarrassed looks on the faces of those national guards.

What was mud? Under the circumstances, none of us cared about a little dirt. For that matter, what was sleep? Time had stopped for all of us.

And what was food? Food was just a necessary nuisance. It appeared in abundance at our house and at the houses of my aunts and uncles. There was so much food, in fact, that we transported much of it to the search sites where the National Guard had set up tents with tables and hot coffee.

Each night when we returned home, there was always a new supply of food. In our small house with its miniscule kitchen, food was stacked everywhere.

Ellen O'Shields couldn't bear to go to the search site for her first-born child. She stayed busy in her Atlanta home greeting visitors and caring for her three youngest children. One of her sons worked part-time at a farmer's market. He was allowed to bring home any produce left over from the day's sales. Ellen would make pots of vegetable soup and send them to the river. It became a favorite of the searchers and guardsmen.

It's not like we didn't have every resource of the times available to us. The Governor of the State of Georgia saw to that. He had been made aware first-hand of our needs in the search by a humble, mild-mannered Claude O'Shields—a man who never imagined that he would enter the Georgia Capitol and ask to speak to the highest elected official in the state: Marvin Griffin, the seventy-second governor of the State of Georgia, from 1955 to 1959.

But his son was missing, and there was nothing he wouldn't do to bring him home. The generating water was a constant source of anguish for our families. It made rescue difficult to impossible, and it created dangerous conditions for the searchers.

A typical day for the rest of us up on the river could be pretty boring. There was no news either way in the search. When the weather was very bad, Lynn and I were required by our mother to stay in a car or to hang out at one of the National Guard tents. If we had been a little older, we could have accompanied some of our aunts. They would walk for miles up and down the riverbanks looking for any signs or clues. It would rain and their clothes would get soaking wet. Then their clothes would turn to ice.

They even followed the railroad tracks from one point on the river to another. Once they wandered into a pasture because farms were all along the river. Dorothy remembers someone hollering, "Here comes a bull!" She had a red scarf on. She yanked the scarf off as she ran for a fence. She scaled the fence in one leap.

Porta-potties came into general use in the 70s. It seems all kinds of modern conveniences came into being *after* we could have used them.

So we would have to drive back into Cartersville to a gas station. Or find a secluded place out in the woods. One day, Aunt Athaleen and Aunt Dorothy took Lynn and me to a spot out in the middle of nowhere. We're out of the car when Aunt Athaleen looks up at this *enormous* tree and spots some mistletoe at the very top. Because all the leaves on the tree had dropped, it stood out like a shiny, green lantern.

She says to Dorothy, "Now that's about the finest bunch of mistletoe I've ever seen in my life. I believe you and me can climb up this tree and bring it down." Dorothy says nothing and Aunt Athalene repeats, "I believe we can. I believe we can."

I didn't want to be the one to have to tell the rest of the family about another catastrophe. I was looking back at the car, trying to determine whether I could drive the car back to the camp for help when the two of them fell out of that tree and broke their necks. It didn't matter whether the car was an automatic or a stick, I was still only eleven, and my short legs probably wouldn't have reached the pedals anyway.

Finally, I heard Dorothy saying, "I believe we can, too. But it's late and starting to get dark. We better head back."

From my viewpoint, these two aunts had always been complete opposites: Athaleen the "risk everything for fun" one, Dorothy "the voice of reason." Thank God, she talked Athaleen out of the crazy deed. I breathed a sigh of relief.

12

The Search - Day 7
Thursday, December 5

Searchers to Block Etowah

*Steel mesh will be strung across the Etowah River at strategic points
Wednesday in an effort to turn up two Atlanta area duck hunters who
have been missing since last Friday.*

*Bartow County Sheriff Frank Atwood said Tuesday night that after
the mesh has been installed, the Allatoona Dam generators will be
run at maximum force. He said the generators, which have been
idle for the past three days, will raise the Etowah's water level about
6–10 feet.*

*The missing men, Earl Rich of Smyrna and Albert O'Shields of
Atlanta, are employees of Atlantic Steel.*

The Atlanta Constitution

At the river that morning, Col. Horace Clary of the Rome National
Guard Unit, put his hands on my mother's shoulders as he gave her some
disquieting news. She looked fearful and was holding back tears. He
said quietly, "Now, Mrs. Rich, I promise you we will be back as soon
as we clear up the problem over in Villa Rica."

What the "problem in Villa Rica" meant for my family was this:
the National Guard Unit helping with the search for my father was
pulled to assist with the recovery of the bodies in the nearby massive
gas explosion. In the days before Middle East crises, the National Guard
actually "guarded the nation"—which in many cases meant these grisly
assignments.

Explosion Rips Four Villa Rica Stores
At Least Eight Persons Killed With Unknown
Number Trapped

A gas explosion believed to have been caused by a faulty gas heater wrecked four stores today, killing at least eight persons, and trapping an unknown number in the wreckage.

A city policeman said there might have been as many as 40 to 50 persons in the four stores when the explosion happened. Twenty people were taken to a local hospital with injuries. Some were reported badly burned.

The stores included a drug store, a 10-cent store, and a jewelry store. Bill Berry, owner of the drug store where the explosion occurred at 11:00 a.m., said two men were working on a faulty gas breaker at the time. Both men are missing. He identified them as O.T. Dyer and his son Johnny. Berry's wife was also among the missing.

The body of Dr. Jack Burnham, who had an office over the drug store, was recovered. Two patients in his office have not been found.

The stores were located at U.S. Highway 78, the Birmingham-Atlanta Highway. A wall of the drug store came crashing down on several cars parked nearby. Fires that followed the explosion were brought under control an hour and a half later. Fire Departments from Atlanta, 37 miles eastward and from other communities rushed to the scene.

The Daily Tribune News
Cartersville, Georgia

Villa Rica, another sleepy little Southern town, is located thirty-seven miles due west of Atlanta.

If you had a perfect triangle, Atlanta and the bedroom communities, which play heavily in the parts of this story, would look like this:

Cartersville

Marietta

Smyrna

Villa Rica   Atlanta

Mother was stricken with concern, of course, for the victims in Villa Rica, probably more so than she would have been just a day or so earlier when the reality of tragedy had come crashing down on us. But her focus was on finding my father, plain and simple.

Just as my dad had set out on a seemingly normal day to do what he had done hundreds of times before, so too, the people of Villa Rica were going about their normal business on a weekday: going to the store or to the dentist, seeing to some early Christmas shopping. Some were out to cast their ballots in a municipal election going on at the time. And in an instant, lives were gone and many others were changed forever.

Eyewitnesses said clothing, papers, wood, bricks, and other debris fell from the sky like rain. One man in the drugstore who lived to tell about it, Ralph Fuller, had to be pulled from the wreckage. He received severe burns in the blast and was hospitalized. Although he has no memory of how long he was in the hospital, he did remember the reaction of family members who visited him there. "My own sister didn't recognize me from the burns I had," Mr. Fuller said.

James Harrison, a long-time pharmacist, missed the explosion by seconds. He had been out making house calls with a doctor friend and had returned to the town just before 11:00 a.m. His friend dropped him off in front of Berry's Pharmacy.

Harrison started inside to have a soft drink, but suddenly remembered that it was Election Day. He walked away to the voting site. Just as he reached it, the explosion occurred, destroying Berry's Pharmacy and two other stores.

The following persons perished in the December 5, 1957 natural gas blast in downtown Villa Rica:

Mrs. Ann Pope Smith, age 23
Mrs. Margaret Berry
Bobby Roberts, age 13
Miss Carolyn Davis, age 22
Oscar Hixon, age 34
O.T. Dyer, age 60
Johnny Dyer, age 30
Rob Broom, age 54
Dr. Jack Burnham, a dentist
Kenneth Hendrix
Carl Vinter
Rozella Johnson

Two people were missing in Cartersville: Daddy and Albert. Over a dozen were dead in Villa Rica. Like Mother, I wondered if the math was going to work against us in the search for Daddy. Though many civilian volunteers remained, it seemed eerily quiet at the river with the guardsmen gone.

13

The Search - Day 8
Friday, December 6

Villa Rica Wreckage Gives up Bodies of 17; Business Section in Rubbles
Four Stores Are Demolished; 20 to 30 Persons Injured

The Daily Tribune News
Cartersville, Georgia

Unlike the seemingly endless search for my father, the Villa Rica tragedy was, at least logistically, wrapped up rather quickly, and the National Guard returned to the site of the Etowah River in Cartersville, Bartow County, Georgia.

On this same date, the newspaper carried the following story about our search:

Volunteers Needed to Search Etowah

Volunteers are needed for Saturday to continue the search for the bodies of the two duck hunters missing since last Friday.

The water will be at low ebb on Saturday morning so an intensive search is being launched for the bodies.

Sheriff Frank Atwood asked all volunteers to be at the Milam Bridge at 9 o'clock Saturday and they will be assigned stations up and down the river in order that the entire river may be carefully watched from banks, boats, and bridges.

The Daily Tribune News
Cartersville, Georgia

The Search - Day 9
Saturday, December 7

December weather in this part of the South can be either beautiful or nasty this time of year. Unfortunately, today it is the latter. Mother has left us at the house. There must be ten friends and neighbors here to watch us though, including my maternal grandmother, Frances Reed, and my mother's only sibling, Betty Reed Kikendall.

Aunt Betty married a man from Illinois whom she met when he was stationed at Dobbins Air Force Base in our area. After their marriage, they moved to a strange, otherworld place called Chicago. Once my dad went missing, Uncle Bob brought Aunt Betty back to Georgia to be with her only sister. She had been here a week.

Now it is time for her to return to Illinois. She had her own small children to tend to, after all. Nobody had any idea how long the search would go on. She would hug us until we could hardly breathe, then cry all the way out the driveway until we lost sight of her car.

But before she left on this Saturday morning, some reporters would arrive unannounced at the house and ask to take pictures of Lynn and me holding a portrait of our dad. My grandmother and aunt said, "Come right in."

The reporters also went to the river and interviewed Mother, but they failed to mention to her that they had already been to the house. Later, when Mother returned home for the day, we met her at the door saying, "Guess what, Mother. The newspaper people took our picture!"

She didn't say anything out loud about the reporters' visit to our home, but she had her telltale straight-lipped "I'm not happy" expression on her face. That's how we always knew she was displeased. Her "cupie doll" mouth became a perfectly level straight line.

Mother was always a very private person. Her motto was always, "We don't air our laundry in public." I can only imagine that she felt she was losing control of, not just her family, but her entire world. Her husband was lost and her children had become public spectacles. She was unable to fix anything or protect any of us.

That one incident remains a cherished memory to Lynn and me—a little excitement to break the misery. We put on our best dresses and sat on the sofa holding one of our dad's Navy portraits. When I looked down at it, though, I almost broke out in tears. How handsome my dad was and how happy he looked! I had not seen him in over a week. It seemed like an eternity.

How can I describe Daddy's physical appearance? Probably the first thing you would notice about him was his "grin." His smile revealed the most perfect set of teeth you've ever seen, yet he never visited a dentist until he went into the Navy. Lynn has the same teeth and grin. Judy got the grin but not the teeth. Me, I have his round face.

Physically, he was just short of six feet tall, big boned, with very sharp facial features, *extremely* blue eyes, light red wavy hair, and fair skin.

He sported tattoos on each arm of naval sailing vessels of old, complete with massive sails. One of them also included the words, "U.S. Navy." Tattoos in the 1940s did not carry the same connotation of our modern day, that of being mainstream and trendy. They were reserved for rebels, military men, and circus performers.

He rarely wore a shirt when he worked outdoors, leading to a complete covering of freckles. He had gained the nickname of "Pinky" and now nobody seems to know where it came from. One theory is that Papa Rich gave it to him because he made up funny names for all his kids—and this, his fifth-born, had red hair.

Still another theory is that he got the name "Pinky" in the Navy. Onboard ships in the Atlantic and Pacific, sailors often went without shirts on the hot decks, and his sunburns became legendary. At any

PHYLLIS RICH CARPENTER

rate, when motorcycles drove up in our driveway looking for my dad to work on their engines, I knew whom they meant when they asked if "Pinky" was home.

Daddy had a raspy voice, whereas Mother had a rather glamorous, Hollywood-type voice. All three of us girls inherited our father's raspy voice. We sound so similar on the phone, it is sometimes difficult for even acquaintances to tell us apart.

In terms of personality, Daddy was the happiest person I've ever known. But you didn't want to rile him. If he came to feel he couldn't trust you, he could turn on a dime and become your worst enemy.

14

The Search - Day 10
Sunday, December 8

Lynn and I were pictured on the front page of the *Atlanta Journal-Constitution* holding Daddy's smiling Navy portrait with the caption: "Lynn and Phyllis Rich Wait at Home." This story followed:

Families Await Outcome of Grim Etowah Dragging
Tots to Face Bleak Yule

Two little girls stayed at home in Smyrna Saturday, trying hard to keep their minds on Christmas and Santa Claus and all the nice things that happen to children this time of year.

But mostly eleven-year-old Phyllis Rich and her blond-haired little sister, nine-year-old Lynn, were thinking about their daddy.

Forty miles north of Smyrna, on the banks of the angry-looking Etowah River near Cartersville, the little girls' mother kept up her constant vigil—her thoughts, too, on the children and their father.

She stared silently at the swirling water and waited with a mixture of hope and dread for word that searchers had recovered the body of her husband.

All hope had been wrung from her that her husband, thirty-five-year-old Earl Rich, might still be alive. Still she stayed and watched as search parties probed the Etowah.

It had been eight days since Mr. Rich—who all his life had loved to hunt and fish—and a companion, Albert O'Shields, 25, of Holly Street, Atlanta, were last seen while on a duck hunting trip on the Etowah.

Discovery of the hunters' overturned boat indicated
drowned. But as the days passed, the dark waters stubb
to give up the bodies.

The search goes on daily by National Guardsmen and volunte
the Atlantic Steel Co. in Atlanta where the two men worked.

And each day the wives and other members of the two families gather
at the river's edge to watch the searchers go out in boats to plumb the
depths of the river with grappling hooks.

A huge net spans the river at Hardin's Bridge 10 miles northwest of
Cartersville to keep the bodies from passing that point.

* * *

On most days, Lynn and Phyllis join their mother in her lonely vigil.
But Saturday it was too cold and rainy. So they remained at home at
106 Adams St. in Smyrna with relatives and friends. Other relatives
were keeping their eight-month-old sister, Judy.

"The two little girls were so anxious for Christmas to get here," said
their aunt, Mrs. Betty Kikendall. "They wanted Santa Claus to bring
them a new television set."

"We're going ahead with our Christmas plans," she said. "Their
mother wants it that way."

* * *

At the riverbank, Mrs. Rich spoke softly as she huddled in a car and
watched the searching party in the boats.

"We know the men are dead," she said. "But we'll keep coming here
until they find the bodies. We'll never be satisfied until they find them."

The search was being carried out on Saturday at Milam Bridge, a few miles
below where the two men were known to have begun their hunting trip.

Downstream, Claude E. O'Shields, of Center Hill, father of Albert
O'Shields, stood warming himself by a fire at Hardin's Bridge near
the 75-foot net.

He said he and his daughter-in-law, along with other relatives had been at the scene from daylight to dark almost every day but that his missing son's wife had been persuaded to stay home Saturday.

Mr. and Mrs. O'Shields have no children.

Both the missing men are from large close-knit families and their brothers and sisters have come to the riverbank almost every day, Mr. O'Shields said.

Mr. Rich's mother, Mrs. H.R. Rich, resides in Marietta. His three brothers and seven sisters all live there, too.

Mr. O'Shields has five brothers and a sister. His parents reside at 949 N. Grand Ave., NW, in Center Hill.

Atlanta Journal-Constitution

At no time did my mother tell Lynn and me that she felt "the men are dead," even the night of The Talk. But she did speak about her fears with some of her friends, including Marlene Wilbur. Marlene recalls that Pat said, "I cannot tell the children he's dead because he's a good swimmer and I have absolutely no proof that he is dead."

"And then," Marlene continues, "she was really telling herself the same thing."

We would have reacted negatively if she had acted as if he were not coming home. He was lost, maybe, but not dead. Or perhaps he was being held against his will. In time, he would outwit his captors. We were not willing to accept an unhappy ending.

PHYLLIS RICH CARPENTER

The Search - Day 11
Monday, December 9

Families Keep Vigil As Search Continues For Missing Hunters

Despite the fact that Sunday was the tenth day since Earl Rich and Albert O'Shields disappeared beneath the surface of the Etowah River, not a trace of the bodies of these men had been found, Sheriff Frank C. Atwood announced.

Mr. C. E. O'Shields, father of one of the victims and two of his surviving sons, spent another day of vainly searching the banks Sunday, just as they have every day since the search began ten days ago.

Mrs. H. R. Rich, mother of victim Earl Rich, who resides on Canton Road north of Marietta, also spent all day Sunday at the Hardin Bridge, along with members of her family, including two daughters and a son.

Hundreds of persons motored to the Hardin Bridge area south of Kingston and to the Milam Bridge area in the Euharlee community. And a vigil and search was being maintained along both sides of the river banks as well as in deep holes of the river itself, but no trace of the bodies was available.

Only the boat in which they started out on what they had hoped would be a day of duck hunting on the river together with both paddles have been retrieved. One of the paddles was located several miles downstream from the Hardin Bridge.

Fears have been expressed that the bodies of the two men may have become trapped in some deep crevice, and that the passing surges of water have heaped mud and debris upon them to the extent a rising to the surface by the bodies is out of the question.

On the other hand, stories are being related by those who have searched records of river tragedies to the effect that bodies have been found as much as forty and sixty miles downstream two months after they disappeared beneath the water's surface.

*The Daily Tribune News
Cartersville, Georgia*

I had been reading the newspaper daily since I was five or six. But now someone at our house was "collecting" the papers each day, perhaps so we couldn't read such dire predictions.

Mother is making us go back to school for the week. We already missed one week, but in just one more week, school will be out for Christmas holidays.

Learning has been a lifelong joy for me. And reading? Well, one summer I read nearly every book in the tiny one-room library in our town of Smyrna. When the little old lady librarian, Ms. Mazie Nelson, would see me coming, she was scrambling to find me something new to read.

But that was *before*. Now I could see no use for any of it. I spent the whole week staring at the door to my classroom, convinced that at any moment, someone would come from the office with the good news that my daddy had been found safe and sound. Or bad news. How would I be able to handle that in front of all my friends?

Today's young people are part of a transient generation. They will never have what I have, which is to say lifelong friends. They are the same friends who have known me since I was five years old, who lived with me through those difficult days while my father was missing. Even now when I run into them, their first words to me are, "I still remember when your dad was lost."

Actually, young people are good at comforting other young people. My friends didn't make me feel awkward, didn't ask me unnecessary questions, and didn't stop me if I needed to talk. Still, they didn't and couldn't know that I could appear happy and normal on the outside, but that I was actually screaming on the inside. But even when I had my ups and downs, they were not judgmental.

During the search, many of my friends and their parents either called our home or came by to visit. And, of course, they brought food. One friend, Cathy, remembers clearly coming to my house, but being told by her mom before they came, "Now, don't say anything to Phyllis about her dad."

Lynn remembers her teacher and some of her classmates bringing Christmas presents to our house to put under the tree that someone decorated for us. She remembers opening one, a color book and crayons. Our whole community was heart-broken for us and we could see that and feel that. It helped, but what we really wanted was our dad back.

The Search - Day 13
Wednesday, December 11

Vigil on Etowah Is Held Up For Remainder of the Week
$200 In Reward Money Offered For Recovery of Two Bodies

Because searchers are exhausted from a 10-day vigil kept along the Etowah River banks for several miles along that stream, the search has been held up for the remainder of the week, Sheriff Frank C. Atwood announced from his office Wednesday morning.

Meanwhile, the full force of the waters turned loose through the generators at Allatoona Dam will be allowed to run in the belief that the continued force might dislodge the bodies of the victims, which may be trapped in some hole or under logs at the bottom of the river.

The fellow workers of O'Shields and Rich at the Atlantic Steel Company have offered cash rewards of $100 for the recovery of each of the two men.

Up to 2:30 Wednesday afternoon, not one single trace other than the locating of the boat and paddles used by the men where they started out on their ill-fated trip have been found, Sheriff Atwood informed the Tribune News.

The Daily Tribune News
Cartersville, Georgia

Throughout the long search, Sheriff Frank Atwood of Cartersville won the trust and respect of our family. Uncle Esco would say of him, "Sheriff Atwood was a dandy. He was down there every day getting muddy just like everybody else: rangers, deputies, National Guard, navy divers, private divers. Dynamite. Airplanes. The Steel Plant, where your daddy and Albert O'Shields worked, 'bout had to close down."

The newspaper also announced on this date that a cold wave would be dipping the mercury into the teens, as low as sixteen degrees. Included would be snow flurries whirled by winds reaching twelve miles an hour. None of this would stop our search or vigil, but made it all that more miserable.

Just the weekend before Thanksgiving, the weather had been warm and beautiful. We had taken a family day-trip to North Georgia to view the sights around *another* river, the Tallulah River. At least several weekends out of every month, my dad loved nothing more than to get in the car and take off to all our state's natural wonders. Perhaps the travel bug bit him during his WWII world travels. He had an insatiable curiosity.

The Tallulah River formed a gorge two miles long and one thousand feet deep, sort of a "mini Grand Canyon." Visitors can hike to the gorge floor unless water is being released from the river dam. A suspension bridge sways 80 feet above the rocky bottom.

Tightrope walkers have twice crossed the gorge, one being Karl Wallenda of the famous "Flying Wallendas." It was on July 18, 1970, and he was sixty-five years old. An estimated thirty thousand people watched Wallenda perform two headstands as he crossed the quarter-mile-wide gap. The towers he erected for that stunt are still present today.

The Tallulah River is not part of the Etowah River system, but rather The Tallulah intersects with the Chattooga River to form the Tugaloo River at Lake Tugaloo in Habersham County. It joins South Carolina's Seneca River at Lake Hartwell to create the Savannah River, which flows southeastward into the Atlantic Ocean.

I would say the day at the Tallulah Gorge and River was the best day ever, but our lives were filled with "best" days. We had lunch at the little gift shop and Daddy bought us little plastic Indian princess dolls, a nod to the Cherokee Indian heritage of the area. I still have my little doll.

15

How are you gonna' keep 'em down on a Georgia farm after they've seen:

New York City
Miami
California
Brazil
Trinidad
Philippine Islands
Cuba
Mexico
Ellice Islands
Marshall Islands
Saipan
Guam
Caroline Islands
North Africa
Amazon River
Other "top secret" locations

My grandmother, Mama Rich, had kept each of the dozens of her son Earl's letters home from World War II. Reading these letters is like having an intimate conversation with my father—the young version of him with all his hopes and dreams.

After Papa Rich's death, my father slipped into the role of "patriarch" of the family. He didn't ask for the role; it just came his way. His older brother Esco was eccentric and a little unpredictable, but for sheer entertainment purposes, Esco was your man. Dad was more serious. Besides, like the young men of his generation, Daddy had gone to war as a boy but returned a man older and wiser than his years.

The US Navy organized the Submarine Chaser Training Center in Miami in April of 1942 in a desperate attempt to combat the relentless

German U-boat threat. U-boats were wreaking havoc all along the US east coast in the months after Pearl Harbor while sinking an average of a ship per day.

Daddy was sent to the school in May of 1942, and his was one of the first classes to graduate from the school. The very colorful Lt. Eugene McDaniel (Annapolis 1927) became the commanding officer of the training facility.

The commander placed a bullet-riddled, bloodstained wooden lifeboat out in front of the facility to drive home the point of whom they were battling. Lt. McDaniel had seen, firsthand, helpless merchant sailors who had been machine-gunned by Nazis U-boat skippers.

After his ninety days' training, Daddy was assigned to PC-489, one of the first ten PC ships built and launched. He was basically thrown into a storm that was to be the vanguard of the Allied counter to the "U-boat threat" of 1942. The PC-489 would not only hunt German U-boats, but would also protect merchant vessels along the way. That was their mission as they left New York in July of 1942.

Were these U-boats an idle threat to the United States? Hardly. German U-123 sneaked to within a mile or so of New York Harbor, and its kapitan snapped night photographs of the glowing lights of Manhattan! England was already well acquainted with the threat. Winston Churchill wrote that his only real concern of the war was the "U-boat threat" that nearly strangled Britain into submission by depriving them of much-needed supplies.

PC was short for "Patrol Craft," and that designation was applied to the class of ships designated as small "sub-hunting" ships that were smaller than a destroyer and less than 180 feet in length. PC ships were not given a name but rather numbers, just like the PT boats that included the infamous PT-109. The PCs were bigger than a PT boat, yet somehow the PT boat (Patrol Torpedo) got the *sexy, adventurous* label.

As a matter of fact, PC crews affectionately called their ships the "Donald Duck Navy." They took offense, however, when big-ship sailors used the expression as one of ridicule. Secretly, the big ship sailors must have marveled at the accomplishments of the smaller ships as they bobbed up and down in the big, bad ocean. Although my dad may have preferred to be on a larger ship, it is clear looking back in history the huge role these small ships played in the victory. And the tiny quarters and small crews helped them develop a team spirit that did not always exist on larger ships.

At their training schools, the men were being watched and evaluated as to their particular skills. No surprise to anyone who knew him, Daddy was to become a Gunner's Mate. I'm certain his skills were put to good use. The PCs found plenty of combat action and at closer range to the enemy than if they had been on larger ships.

Lots of people are interested in the history of these ships and their crews and have gone to great lengths to preserve their legacy. My father's pictures are identified on one such site:

http://www.navsource.org/archives/12/010489.htm

Towards the end of his enlistment, Daddy was on a "Liberty Ship"— the USS *Giraffe*, IX118. They were mass-produced and all looked the same from a visual standpoint. You can't tell one from another from a thousand yards away. There are two original examples anchored at Fisherman's Wharf in San Francisco.

Some were built to haul cargo, some were built to carry troops, and some were built to carry oil and aviation fuel (like the USS *Giraffe* and her sisters). So while they looked the same on the outside, their insides were altered to meet their military purpose. The prefix "IX" in translated US Navy terms means "Unclassified Miscellaneous", which is like calling your dog a "mutt."

Having read about life aboard a PC Ship, my nephew Shane believes his grandfather must have thought himself in heaven when he saw the bunks and personal space afforded him on the *Giraffe* versus what he endured on PC-489.

I'm not sure my father even realized how valuable his service on these vessels was at the time. But from the looks of things now, without the efforts of these ships and their small crews, many believe that Americans might now be speaking German. Or Japanese. Or both.

In a letter home from the war in 1942, at his SCTC training in Miami, it is clear Daddy was loving Miami. He wrote:

> Mom, I thought New York was pretty but you just ought to see Miami. We are stationed right in the city and the ocean comes right up in town. There are palm trees everywhere and plenty of oranges and coconuts. The buildings are painted orange or yellow. Really, this is the prettiest place I have seen yet. I have already been in about 18 states and I wouldn't care if they left me here and forgot about me.

In June and July 1942, Daddy was stationed in New York City while the PC-489 was readied for service. And his fascinating assignment at the time was guarding the damaged SS *Normandie*. Formerly a luxury French ocean liner, the *Normandie* was being readied to serve as a US wartime transport ship when it became victim to an accidental fire, or perhaps sabotage. (See YouTube link in Epilogue). He wrote home:

> I have been standing guard on Pier 88 keeping people off of the *Normandie*. It attracts a lot of attention and we have to keep people away from it. She must have been a beauty before she caught fire and burned. They gave us a loaded Colt 45 automatic and a belt full of cartridges, so I guess you can see that we are not guarding her for fun. We have as much authority as the Chief of Police in New York while we are on guard. I have carried a belt and pistol so much 'til I feel like Buffalo Bill Cody. All I need is a horse and saddle.

He also partied at *The Stage Door* with an actress named Hope White and met Jack Dempsey at his restaurant at Broadway and Forty-Second Street. These were eye-opening experiences for a young Georgia man raised on a farm!

About this same time, he also wrote the following words home to his mom and dad from his naval assignment in Brooklyn:

> Say, we had a murder or something up here. Yesterday two bodies were washed ashore about a hundred yards from the station. You could see them from the back window. I don't know whether they were killed or fell overboard from a ship and drowned. Anyway, some seem to think they have been dead a long time.

From July 14 to October 13, 1943, Daddy was based in Recife, Brazil. His ship escorted other ships from Trinidad, Recife, and Bahia. It once sailed up the Amazon for repairs. As a gunner's mate, he manned the portside 20-mm Oerilkon Cannon (see YouTube link in Epilogue). Ironically, though, he was an anti-aircraft gunner in the one place where he could never possibly see an enemy aircraft!

The Oerilkon Cannon must have been like a new toy for Daddy. Young American men from backwoods' communities learned to shoot before they entered grammar school. They would become the German and Japanese forces' worst nightmare.

Back on his ship in September 1942 after being hospitalized for tonsillitis, he took part in a depth-charge attack.

> Say Mom, we had a little bit of excitement bringing a convoy back from Key West. We got a Sub. At least, I think we did and the Captain said we did. We picked it up on the sound equipment and dropped six depth bombs on it. The water was covered with oil in about two minutes. Anyway, we chalked it up among the 'missing.'

On February 5, 1943, one of Daddy's good friends and shipmates, Calvin Ray Athy, died in Brazil. After failing to return from shore leave, his body was found floating near his ship. It is unknown as to whether it was accidental or if he was murdered. He was just nineteen. His death would weigh heavily on Daddy's mind, and he would make several trips over the next year to visit Athy's family in San Pedro, California.

In April 1943, Daddy had a ten day leave to visit home. Sometimes he would take buddies from the ship home with him, and vice versa. One, George Renfro, later wrote Mama Rich a letter in which he said, "You can adopt me if you want 'a."

By June 1943, things were heating up between Daddy and my mother, with whom he had been corresponding. He wrote home to his mother, "Pat's small but she's got brains." Just what every girl wants to hear! There's some truth to "a girl in every port" and he would write about some of these girls occasionally. But for the most part, he was shy about personal matters, even with his family. He became irritated when his mother informed him that a girl from home, Myrtle, had told the family she was going to marry him.

> Mama, I didn't pay too much attention when you said that Myrtle told Martha that I asked her to marry me. But now I have received a bunch of letters and almost everyone mentions it. I can tell the truth when I say I didn't say it. So you and the folks just forget about it. I may be crazy but not that crazy.

A few months later, he learned that Myrtle had married someone named Jack and again Daddy wrote home:

> So Myrtle is married, huh? Well, she got a good guy. I have known him for several years and he is a fine fellow. Maybe she will try to be somebody now. I guess the war has just started for Jack!

In August 1943, he volunteered for a "ride-along" on a submarine and looked through the periscope.

> Say, Mom, now get a grip on yourself. I volunteered for a trip on a submarine yesterday and it was about the biggest thrill I've ever had. I looked through the periscope several times and could see the ships looking and hunting for us. We could hear them every time they came over us. It's so quiet down under the water. It seems as if you're sitting still. I can hardly keep from putting in my exam for submarines. I may one day.

He clearly wanted to be on a sub but his parents objected. *They feared that if he was killed at sea, his body would never be found.*

In late November, early December 1943, Daddy was assigned to a new ship and was being sent to the Pacific Theatre. He traveled cross-country to San Pedro, California. There he visited the home of his friend, Calvin Athy, his friend who died in Brazil. He wrote home about the visit:

> I went up to visit Mrs. Athy, Calvin Ray Athy's mother. You remember he was the little curly headed boy in the group picture on the ship with the tattoos on his arms. He was killed or drowned in port.
>
> She is the sweetest woman. She is a lot like you. She about worried herself to death not knowing how her son died until I came here. Mom, I actually believe I helped a lot, including her little daughter, about eight years old. She has another son who's 17 that is for all the world just like Calvin, the one we buried in South America. Write to her, Mom, will you? You could help her a lot. It was pitiful when I answered her questions about Calvin's death. She cried and so did her little girl. But I know she feels a lot better now. At least she knows he had a decent burial.

Once assigned to the USS *Giraffe* (formerly called the USS *Dole*) as GM1C, it was clear that he had matured and learned much. He had to get all the ship's guns in working order. No fear. He never met a gun he couldn't take apart and reassemble. He was also in charge of all the gunner's mates on board.

> Gosh, Mom, I've been so busy since I came aboard my new ship 'til it's simply pitiful. I'm the head Gunners Mate, you know and they look to me for everything. I've been trying to get all the guns together and see about all the other new guns we've ordered. It's almost got me down. I'll catch up sometime, though, and I hope it's soon.
>
> This ship is simply loaded with anti-aircraft guns. You ought to see me (a big shot) boss 'my men' around. Wish Esco could see me now. He'd see what I mean when I tell him I give orders around here!

For most of 1944, he was involved in or at least very near some of the fiercest fighting in the Pacific of the entire war. One of his locations was Peleliu, shown graphically in Ken Burns' "The War." It was the setting of one of the bitterest battles of the war, especially for the Marines, who suffered over 6,500 casualties during one month—over one-third of their entire division. The battle was part of an offensive, which ran most of 1944 in the Pacific Theater of Operations. Both land and naval battles were fought fiercely so I am certain my dad got his chance to "take a crack" at the enemy, which was his wish.

American military men quickly learned the "fight to the death" devotion of Japanese soldiers. One Japanese soldier, Hiroo Onoda, trained in guerilla tactics, hid out on a Philippine island for 29 years after the end of the war! Still believing the war was not over, he was persuaded to surrender in 1974 by a Japanese delegation and family members. He died back in Japan in early 2014 at the age of 91.

Daddy wrote home about the danger he was in from forces of this ardent enemy:

> I know this is going to be a tough trip and I can't keep you from worrying. But don't worry any more than you have to. Just say to yourself that I'm okay and if you don't hear from me for some time, don't give up hope. I always was lucky.

He never noted his whereabouts in writing while in the Pacific due to the fact that the censors would not allow them to mention whereabouts or other battle information. He wrote home:

> I can't tell you where I am or where I'm going except that now I'm somewhere in the southwest Pacific. The censors are pretty strict. The only thing that matters, I suppose, is that I am well and happy. Maybe now I'll be able to get a crack at 'those fellows.'

Some places my dad's ships took him are not part of the record, being secret at the time. But he would sometimes write in tiny letters under the postage stamp to give his family back home a clue. This also hid the info from censors. Every letter my grandmother kept was missing the stamp!

His second ship bounced around, from atoll to atoll, refueling war ships as they "island hopped" towards Japan. The *Giraffe* would trail about 100 miles behind the main body of the fleet and then individual ships would drop back to the *Giraffe* to receive diesel or aviation fuel. Daddy arrived in the Philippines the day the Hiroshima atomic bomb was dropped and never got assigned to another ship.

Immediately after the end of the war, Hollywood churned out one WWII movie after another. Of course, they did not strive to portray the reality of the war, a la *Saving Private Ryan* or *Schindler's List*. They were pure entertainment, and my dad took us to see them all.

Daddy loved the movies and we went to the local drive-in theater at least once a week—sometimes twice—no matter what the weather. His favorite movie of the time (and mine) was *Mr. Roberts* with Henry Fonda. I can remember us laughing hysterically as the drunken naval seaman drove his stolen motorcycle off the pier after a wild shore liberty!

Since he never talked to any of us about his wartime experiences, I remember only a few of his stories, and they were captured by accident. I was not meant to hear them. We took a family vacation to Oklahoma. There we visited with his Oklahoma war-time buddy and his wife, Alva Lee and Floy Harp, and their boys at their rental place.

The buddy and his family traveled from their home in the summer to work on oil pipeline installation. Then the family would return to their permanent home in the winter. Late at night, when we were supposed to be asleep, I was listening through the door. All the laughter got my attention as they talked about their wartime experiences.

First, they talked about responding to an "all hands on deck." When they got to their battle stations, the whole ocean was on fire. They couldn't even tell the enemy from their own ships, so didn't know where to aim their guns.

The next story took place at some port in the South Pacific. Apparently, "smoke screen" is not just a figure of speech. There really was smoke screen machines used to cover targets from overhead enemy bombers. This particular time that enemy bombers flew over, the Navy personnel were unable to get the machine to work. After the bombers left, the machine suddenly started working and wouldn't shut off. The port was covered in smoke for three days! Daddy and his buddy laughed and laughed over this.

The next story was not a funny one. A young sailor, a gunner, was experiencing his first real sea battle. He panicked and froze at his gun, which was pointed at his crewmates. A number of his own men were killed before the young sailor could be pried from his gun. These are not the things you see in a John Wayne movie.

At the end of the war, men were just plucked off bloody islands, out of cold trenches in Europe, or off battleships with guns still smoking— then deposited back where they came from. Post-traumatic stress disorder was not a term we ever heard in the 1950s. If Daddy suffered from that yet-to-be defined psychosomatic illness, it was not apparent to me. His attitude towards the war was much like his attitude towards life in general. He acted as if his time served had just been one great adventure.

16

My parents were very much in love. There was something so special about the courtships and marriages of the 1940s. Most of the courtships were whirlwind, but the marriages typically lasted for decades.

Mother was almost too young to be a part of that whole scene, but she was a romantic at heart and determined to make it happen. Her older cousin Martha was married to my Uncle Esco. That's why she wrote to his brother, Earl Rich, while he was in the Navy.

When Dad had a leave in New York City, he tried to call my mother at home in Marietta, Georgia. My Grandmother Reed had to tell him that she and some of her friends were attending a swing music concert at the Fox Theater in Atlanta performed by Spike Jones, a sort of renegade of the swing era. Spike Jones' trademark was baggy plaid coats, funny bow ties, and crazy-looking hats. Even his music was bizarre. His "band" played pots and pans, bells, and horns and anything else they could get a sound out of.

Undeterred, Daddy called the Fox Theater and asked to speak to the management. When he explained that he was just home from the war, the manager gratefully had my mom's name printed out on the newsreel being shown on the movie screen prior to the concert. She took Daddy's call in the manager's plush upstairs office at the Fox, a place off-limits to the public. She was extremely impressed with the attention, and if not for that, I might never have been born.

Those wonderful, whirlwind "wartime romances" spawned numerous Hollywood movies featuring the likes of Claudette Colbert, John Wayne, Kirk Douglas, Van Johnson, Ingrid Bergman, and Maureen O'Hara, to name a few.

My maternal grandparents weren't thrilled with the happenings because their daughter was only sixteen. But my mother had made up her mind that she had eyes only for the handsome sailor with the wavy red hair. And about this point in time, Daddy's letters home to his mother took a distinct turn in tone and content. Mama Rich had to know her son's heart had been claimed.

Mother was still a teenager when I was born. She taught me the Jitter Bug before I could walk. She always loved to dance. My parents laughed a lot and seemed to be in total agreement. This is curious since he was a farm boy from a large family and she was an "up-town girl" with just one sister. She had many advantages growing up that my dad didn't have. Even so, her world seemed to revolve around him.

I remember only one real argument, which ironically seems to have been over a trivial thing. For some reason, Daddy criticized Mother's housekeeping. Now this is a mystery to me since Mother was the *ultimate housekeeper, cook, and caretaker*—even during those times when she worked outside our home.

Dad had a mild meltdown and this did not sit well with my mother. After he left for work, she took Lynn and me and we had a "sleepover" at my maternal grandparents' house. It was great fun. Early the next day, my Dad arrived sporting a rather humble expression. Next thing I knew, the sleepover was over, and we were headed back to our house. I never heard Daddy complain about Mother's housekeeping again.

What can we learn from these wartime marriages, which lasted for decades? *They had their priorities in perfect order.* They loved their children and saw to it that they were fed, clothed, and received whatever medical care was available at the time. If you were fortunate, they would tuck you into bed at night and give you a kiss. But we were not the center of their universe. Their spouse was!

We were the children of those romantics, born in the '40s and growing up in the '50s. Some say it was the best time for young people. I can attest that it was never dull.

Whether we like it or not, we are influenced by the politics of our times. My parents grew up knowing the language of World War I. My father wrote home from his stint in the Navy that he might become the next "Sgt. York." My parents and my grandparents alike talked often of the "Great Depression." And it formed the habits of their lives.

I, too, learned the language and signs of the time in which I was born—some good and some more sinister. I knew exactly who Tokyo Rose was. I knew about Emperor Hirohito. I didn't know where Iwo Jima was, but I knew it was a bad place. My dad's friend, Max Hood, was injured there. My mother said he was lucky to get out alive.

There was the "secret trunk" on our enclosed back porch. We weren't allowed to get into it, but Lynn and I would sneak a peek now and then as kids would. There were wooden shoes my dad had bought in the Philippines for my mother. Village scenes were actually carved into the heels of the shoes, then hand-painted in bright colors.

There were pictures of strange, exotic women from Brazil, with little notes to my dad written on the back. My mother said Daddy could speak fairly good Portuguese. He learned the language in Brazil in order to make time with the women. And from the number of photos of Brazilian women in the trunk, he was very popular. Mother seemed to understand. She probably thought, "He can't help it. He is, after all, very good-looking."

There were also the Japanese long-play recordings that were really strange sounding. There were Japanese weapons, carved knives and gross pictures of dead Japanese soldiers surrounded by happy, smiling Navy sailors. Since we weren't allowed to be in the trunk in the first place, I couldn't very well ask Daddy any questions about its contents, but I assume he picked up these souvenirs after some of the battles subsided in the South Pacific islands.

After the war, Daddy never wanted anything Japanese in our house. The funny thing is that when the war ended, absolutely *everything* was "Made in Japan."

I was always listening to the grown-up conversations. From what I gathered, I knew my parents did *not* "Like Ike", although I never knew why. I knew that absolutely nobody liked his wife Mamie's hairstyle. My parents, along with every other American of the time, worshipped Franklin Roosevelt. He could have done no wrong, to hear them tell it.

They were okay with Harry Truman, too. Everyone seemed to think dropping the bomb was a good thing. They agreed with Truman himself when he said the U.S. had used it "to shorten the agony of war."

Nevertheless, bomb talk scared the dickens out of someone my age. We lived near Dobbins Air Force Base, so I would worry about every plane flying over during the night. Would this one drop the bomb? It didn't help that in school we regularly had air raid drills. We were to cover our heads and get under our desks. As if a tiny school desk could save one from a nuclear attack!

We had a clear understanding of what was expected of us as kids in the 1950s. We knew where we fell in the grand scheme of things, which was somewhere way down the totem pole. It was an adult's world. Our parents paid much more attention to each other than they did to us. But we were supposed to give *them* our rapt attention. Once we got to school, teachers were just other adults we were accountable to. We did our own homework and could take credit—or blame—for every grade we earned.

We were allowed to express our opinions (carefully) to our parents or other adults, but they didn't count for much. Feelings? Nobody gave a whit about our self-esteem. We might even be told that we were getting too big for our britches—and they didn't mean it was time to shop for new clothes.

We knew the rules. Or you might could shorten that to "rule." We were to do as we were told. If we forgot "the rule", corporal punishment was allowed and expected. Daddy was a softy most of the time, but a strict disciplinarian when he needed to be. Mother would tell him as soon as he got home if we had done something crazy.

He was consistent and fair. We only got punished when we really deserved it. Sometimes he surprised me. I once brought home a report card on which my teacher wrote a small note on back, "Phyllis talks continuously."

This may have surprised my parents because I was so shy. But I could be a social butterfly with my close friends. I was a nervous wreck as he looked at the note and opened the card. But then he said, "Well, you still managed to get straight As." He never said anything else to me about it.

Life was not without its rewards. Our parents weren't as worried about us, so we got to do things that would probably be frowned upon today. One of those was riding motorcycles. We shared Daddy's passion for them. Mother never made an objection to our riding on motorcycles with our dad. After all, she knew whom she had married.

I know the cycle was a Harley-Davidson, though it would be tough to identify the year or model. He was known to take pieces from several old cycles and custom make his own one-of-a-kind model. And he often had more than one motorcycle at a time. There was an old Indian motorcycle hanging in the garage in 1957, which would probably be worth a fortune today.

My most cherished memory is of Lynn and me riding with him, Lynn on front, me on the back. We would wait at the end of the driveway for him to bring the bike out of the garage. I could feel my heart beating with excitement, almost out of my chest. Just the roar of the engine transported me to another place.

The rules were that I was to hold on tight and hold my short legs out to keep from being burned by the tailpipe. Helmets were unheard of. Shoes were not required. Until flip flops came into being in my early teens, we went barefoot all summer anyway.

These motorcycle excursions were not wimpy rides. Aunt Athaleen described riding on a motorcycle with either Esco or Earl. She said, "They were wild and crazy. Turn a curve and you almost drug the ground!"

The rides I loved the best were the ones at night. Lights from passing cars and buildings would flash by like colored, horizontal ribbons. The wind would rush through your hair. I couldn't hear anything over the roar of the engine, but it was music to my ears. I would look down at the pavement and marvel that it was just inches below my bare feet. Those rides were the closest thing to euphoria I have ever experienced. I wanted them to never end!

One day Daddy asked Lynn if she wanted to ride along on the motorcycle to Uncle Esco's house. She beat him to the motorcycle. At one point during the ride, Daddy pointed to the speedometer. It was dead on 100 mph. Lynn wasn't the least bit afraid. When they got home, Daddy said, "Don't tell your mother." Soon as she was in the door, she said, "Mother, we went 100 miles per hour!"

Baby Judy had already had her first solo ride with Dad in his truck. He took some junk to the dump and she rode along. On the way back, he stopped at Uncle Esco and Aunt Martha's house. Aunt Martha remembers baby Judy grinning from ear to ear in her little seat. Soon she would be ready for her first motorcycle ride. Judy was already becoming a "Daddy's girl," like her two older sisters. My mother had just accepted the inevitable.

All parents could profit from copying my dad's easy style. He never tried to change us from what we were. It was like he was watching a flower bloom or a chic hatch. I think he was sizing up what kind of little people we were and what we would become. I was the "sissy," but he was realizing I wouldn't always be a pushover.

When I was around three, he turned the car over in a ditch on the way to Mama Rich's house. Only Lynn and I were in the car. There was no such thing as car seats, so Lynn and I flew around the car like toys but, fortunately, weren't hurt. Physically, that is. I immediately turned into Indignant Toddler. "Get me out of here," I screamed. "Get me out of this car right now!" To my surprise, he just laughed and said, "Okay. Okay. I'm getting you out!"

He also knew I was prone to take a risk now and again. Probably came by that naturally. Cousin Danny, one of Uncle Esco's sons, was just a few years older than I was and was the brother I never had. I thought he was the coolest person on the planet. Besides his massive, cool comic book collection that would probably be worth a fortune today, he was a talented artist. He drew for hours.

Once he drew freehand several hundred pictures of Donald Duck, just like Disney and pasted them together along one edge. When he flipped through the pages, Donald Duck was running and flapping his wings. He even added his own sound by talking like a duck. At nine or ten, I was awestruck and felt extremely privileged to be able to stand in his presence.

Now, Danny could ride a bicycle without his hands touching the handlebars. It was the most thrilling maneuver I had ever witnessed. We lived in the little house on Adams Drive by then—where we were living when my dad went missing. The road in front of our house went straight downhill, with a little patch of gravel at the bottom.

After Danny demonstrated the no-hands ride, I proclaimed that I could do it, too. This was my first bike and I had learned to ride just the week before. After I hit the gravel patch at the bottom of the hill and crashed, I regained consciousness for a few seconds—just long enough to see Danny running like a jackrabbit towards my house. I guess he was going for help.

I don't recall anything else until Daddy was carrying me up the road, all bloody and bruised. He said, "Why do you think you can do everything that fool Danny does?"

I knew I had scared him, but looking back on it, I just couldn't help it—any more than he could help his temper or his bad language. I was, after all, the daughter of a man who rode a motorcycle with no hands on the bars, standing up on the seat.

It gives me satisfaction to know that my father knew we were tough little girls and had his same fearlessness and sense of adventure.

There were legends about him and his motorcycle antics. But even before he matured, there was a method to his madness. Before Judy was born and while Lynn and I stayed behind with our maternal grandparents, he and my mother were riding a motorcycle to Gadsden, Alabama. They were going to watch some motorcycle races, then stay overnight with her grandparents, the Robertson's—a real date night.

Rounding a curve, Daddy had to lay the cycle down in order to slide under a jack-knifed truck stopped dead in the road. My mother bore an X-shaped scar on her knee for the rest of her life. If not for Daddy's skill, they could have been killed. As it was, they were bruised, cut, and sore. My grandparents and Esco took their cars to Alabama to collect my injured parents after their release from the hospital for the return trip to Georgia.

Daddy convinced Esco to drive him by the body shop in Gadsden to check on his motorcycle. Once there, he told Esco he just wanted to drive it around the block to see how extensive the damage was to the cycle. Mind you, he was so sore he could barely move, but was still able to get up on the seat. Both cars waited for his return. And waited. And waited.

Finally, Uncle Esco said, "We've been had. He's driven that god-damn motorcycle back to Georgia!" The adults seemed to be upset with Daddy for a while, but honestly, even I could have seen that coming, and I was just a child.

Earl and Patricia Rich, 1945

Earl Riley Rich
U.S. Navy, 1944

Patricia Ann Reed
Age 16, 1944

Earl in middle

Earl Rich: The reader in top bunk

Earl Riley Rich on an Indian Bike, 1944

Joseph 'Esco' Rich, U.S. Marines, 1944

*Cousins Danny and Nickie Rich
with Lynn and Phyllis, 1951*

The little house on Adams Drive

Ole Jim

Rich family portrait with the five of us

*Easter 1958: Pat Rich with her girls, left to
right, Lynn, Judy, and Phyllis*

O'Shields Family

Albert O'Shields

Elaine Bullard O'Shields

Elaine and Albert on their wedding day: Feb. 11, 1955

Claude Albert O'Shields was named after his dad
and was a look-alike son.

1952 Graduation from Navy boot camp.
Albert O'Shields shown fourth from right, top row.

Albert's parents: Claude and Ellen O'Shields. They were married in in NY City in 1928. Albert, their first-born, was born July 12, 1932, in Fulton County, Georgia.

1961 O'Shields Family portrait, including Albert's parents, brothers and only sister, Wilhemina: John, Wilhelmina, Dad Claude, Mother Ellen, William, and Carl, along with Wilhemina's small children.

Ellen O'Shields before her death with her five sons, all born after Albert: left to right: John, Carl, James, Robert, William

Milam Bridge: One of the Command Centers

CSX bridge: Launch site

*What the 'walk back' would have looked like
for Earl Rich and Albert O'Shields*

Island trough

Union Calvary Sword Hilt

*December 2012: Judy Rich Whyte with nephew
Scott Oliver at "The Traps" on the Etowah River*

17

Friday, November 29, 1957
The Hunt

Although water was released from both the turbines and the spill gates on November 29, 1957, there was nothing unusual or extreme about the release of water on that day. Nevertheless, fate had begun its steady journey downstream.

The men would have been unable to hear the siren being that far down from the dam, coupled with the noise of the shoals. An hour or so after the release began, the water reached the fish traps, and the level there began to rise—not a "tsunami-like wave" barreling towards them but rather a quick and steady rise.

Initially there is some brief dialogue between the two men. This included the question, "Does it seem like to you that the water is getting higher?"

Upon confirming that the water is indeed rising, the two men would quickly have deduced that the dam was somehow the culprit. The boat was their sole lifeline while on the river, and they would naturally have turned to it as their means of escape in the case of an emergency.

Better to take a long boat ride than to get wet! After all, Earl's truck was waiting for them four miles downriver. Everything that happens next is critical to solving the mystery.

If not yet in panic mode, the men would have thought to gather their equipment to place in the boat prior to getting in the boat themselves. That is, if the boat were on the island with them!

The first objects placed in the boat would have been the guns, because a gun is what each man was holding at that particular moment.

Freeing up both hands would have been the first order of business in order to proceed with launching the boat.

Next, they would have policed up the blind, thermoses, chairs, etc. But moments after these particular events should have taken place, the train engineers had spotted Earl and Albert in the water.

The one and only reason that would explain that the two men were not situated safely in their boat once the threat arose is that there was *no boat to get in to*. If it had been on the island with them, then it was swept away as the water began to rise. If it were on the shore beneath the railroad tracks, then they were trying to get to it.

18

The Search – Day 12
Tuesday, December 10

Nearing the end of nearly two weeks of searching, there is nothing new to be reported by the local newspapers. These are the most frustrating times and the days are long. Each one seems like a month.

Fear was a new emotion for me. We always felt so safe with Daddy. I remember only one time in which he had appeared to be scared himself. It was when our family had an extremely close call: Uncle Jack had barely escaped death when the Navy ship he was on in 1954 had an engine room explosion.

Uncle Jack was just twenty years old and had been in the Navy for two years when the explosion happened. He had been on the US Carrier *Bennington* about seventy-five miles off the coast of Rhode Island, docked at Quonset Point, Rhode Island. On a new assignment in the engine room, Jack had spent two weeks training with a guy named Adams, until he was qualified to run the generators himself. Jack had always stood watch with Adams until the day before the incident. Now they were split up. Jack had just awakened to relieve Adams for chow when the explosion occurred. Adams was the only machinist to get killed.

Uncle Jack was on his top bunk when "general quarters" and fire alarms were sounding. He and the bottom bunkmate thought it was a drill until they smelled smoke and saw it coming through the vents in their sleeping quarters. Jack was dressed and at his station in three minutes. It would normally have been his job to man the OBA (officer's breathing apparatus), but since he was the first one there, he had to put on headset phones. Another sailor arrived and told Jack to continue with the phones. He would handle the OBA—which meant he would have to be in direct contact with the fire and the dead. Uncle Jack said he was glad. The smoke and smell of burning flesh was everywhere.

There had been a hatch on the hangar deck about ten feet square and made of about fourteen inches of thick steel. It was twisted like a pretzel from the heat and pressure of the explosion. There were two explosions on board. To prevent others, men were running with rockets and bombs. Jack saw one dive officer throwing a rocket over the fantail.

The first dead guy Uncle Jack saw was a black man being carried out on a stretcher. His face was burned white. One guy told of a great ball of fire coming at him and knocking him down. The explosion had the force of a shotgun without pellets and it plastered bodies to the walls.

It was believed to have been caused by a cracked starboard catapult line. This was a hydraulic line used to catapult the airplanes taking off the ship so they would clear the ship and not land in the water. It had been under tremendous pressure due to flight operations that morning. The escaping hydraulic oil seeping from the cracked line was under such pressure that when it escaped, it ignited.

At last count, there were 196 dead and 201 injured out of the about 3,000 souls on ship. Many of those were officers. The dead were put on the front hangar deck and covered with sheets. Helicopters ran all day to transport the dead and injured.

Uncle Jack was unaware of the huge vigil back at Mama Rich's house in Marietta, but he was desperately trying to get off the ship long enough to call home. When he finally did, it was hard to find a free telephone line.

Whenever there was a crisis, everyone gathered at Mama Rich's house. She was so worried but scurried around the kitchen trying to stay busy. Daddy knew that Uncle Jack worked in the engine room. Being a Navy veteran himself, he explained to everyone, "When one crew member is on duty, the other is off duty. When one group finishes its watch, the other group comes on. This much we know: the explosion happened about the time of a shift change. So we have a 50/50 chance of Jack being okay. If we get a phone call from the Red Cross or if they come to the house, we're in trouble."

When Uncle Jack called that night, Aunt Dorothy answered the phone. All I heard was clapping, laughing, crying, and screaming. Uncle Jack would be coming home! It was quite some time, though, before my dad seemed his same old, happy self.

In the coming days, the *Atlanta Journal-Constitution* would report, "Two Georgians were killed, and four others injured, two critically, in the explosion and fire aboard the carrier *Bennington*."

If you come from a large family, it increases your odds for tragedy, perhaps. But it also increases your odds for joy and happiness. Why, Uncle Jack's preservation was just more proof to me that we were a blessed family. Everything always turned out well for us.

19

The Search - Day 15
Friday, December 13

The newspaper reports nothing new because the search is stagnant and unfruitful. What does it matter that it's Friday the 13th? It can't get much worse for our family. At least school will be out next week for Christmas holidays.

The search has become our way of life and we have settled into a kind of routine. There is absolutely no thought of giving up the vigil. Lynn and I are holding up pretty well. As long as nothing is found in the river, we continue to be sure that Daddy will be found alive and well. We don't think or talk about any other outcome.

A typical day on the river was to drive back and forth between command centers. There were at least three of them. "Blue Christmas" plays over and over on the car radio, by a newcomer named Elvis Presley whose Christmas album was a new best-seller. He had broken onto the scene the year before with a hit called "Heartbreak Hotel." I never heard my dad voice an opinion about him, one way or another. Daddy was strictly a Johnny Cash fan.

The Search - Day 16
Saturday, December 14

On this day, the weather is cold and windy. Mother leaves us home with the group of ladies that have gathered at our house. Many of Mother's people are from parts of Alabama: Gadsden, Talladega, and Huntsville. This day, her cousin Florene Cline has come over from Talladega, along with her husband, Shorty Cline, and children, Nita Ann and Donny. Shorty went to the river with Mother, who never misses a day no matter what.

Florene stayed at our house. Nita Ann was my age and we have always been the best of friends. We loved to play whenever we were together. Her younger brother, Donnie, was outside with Lynn running around the yard.

Nita Ann came over to me and begged me to go out and play with her. But I couldn't seem to make my feet work. They felt like wet bags of cement as they hung off the sofa. Or my hands. They lay limp in my lap. I had been unable to eat for days. At some point, my mother must have realized it because now it seems people were preparing plates of food constantly and coaxing me to eat. I tried to make them happy, but each bite was torture.

I had to tell Nita Ann I just don't feel like playing. Suddenly she became hysterical, screaming, "I wish he hadn't died! I wish he hadn't died!" Her mother, Florene, rushed her to another room and shut the door. The rest of the visitors in our home remain as they have from the beginning: hushed and motionless—except for those moving food around in the kitchen.

I didn't know what I could do to comfort Nita Ann. I would have liked to assure her that he was not really dead. I was too young to realize that I was paralyzed by grief and fear. So I just sat. But what I really wanted to do was just what Nita Ann had done: *scream to the top of my lungs*.

If we could have gone out to play, it would have been too much to bear to look at the familiar props which had formed my perfect life. Our backyard had always been a noisy scene of activity. Like a mini-farm in the city limits. Daddy had planted every kind of tree you can imagine. Only an orange tree did not survive—too far north—though he gave it a try.

He had much better luck with the grapevines. He made homemade wine from the grapes he picked the summer before. Sometimes the bottles would explode in the middle of the night as they fermented on the back porch. Our whole house would smell like a winery.

We had a swing set—not the Sear's kind, no siree. He built it himself by cementing large rafters into the ground, hanging chain with wooden plank seats. He added a wooden teeter-totter at one end. The swings were so strong, you could practically reach the sky. We knew if we asked for something, it wasn't coming from a store. It would be handcrafted with love. One of Daddy's mottos was, "I'm not paying for anything I can do myself."

Another motto was, "No one leaves my house hungry." This was not difficult for him to carry out since the freezer on the back porch was always full of fish and wildlife Daddy had caught or killed himself. He built a brick grill with a tall smoke stack. He cemented a mailbox in the side for warming bread. I can still taste the barbequed turkey he would serve!

The *Tadpol*, the small wooden boat he built himself, was sitting out back. It was for lakes, not rivers. So he had borrowed one of Uncle Jack's metal boats for his most recent hunting trip. I remember watching him build the *Tadpol*, standing in the hot summer sun sanding down the wood, sweat dripping, and then adding coat after coat of fiberglass.

He deliberately left off the *e* in *Tadpole* because it was one of his dry jokes. He loved pulling people into his private jokes. He laughed every time a stranger came up to him to helpfully point out that he had misspelled the word.

Daddy built pens in the backyard behind the garage to house all the critters he raised for fun, trade, or profit: rabbits, birds, and such. He once sold small chicks to a downtown Marietta store around Easter. When he realized they were dying them pastel colors, he refused to sell to them again.

He had bought an incubator for hatching out the eggs of exotic birds. There was quite a following for these birds, and he made extra money selling them to bird enthusiasts. I remember an egg no bigger than a jellybean. Daddy watched that egg in the incubator for weeks.

One day he came through the kitchen door with his mile-wide grin. "What's up?" we asked. He opened his hand and there was this

PHYLLIS RICH CARPENTER

little bird, no bigger than one of my fingernails. Daddy was completely enamored with the wonder of life.

I guess you could say Daddy was an "animal whisperer." But his favorite animal was Ole Jim. Why, he even named him after his favorite grandfather, Jim Riley Rich, who died before I was born. I don't think Ole Jim was the brightest dog in the world, but I sure wouldn't have told my dad that. He taught Jim to "point" at the prey just like his breed would do at the Westminster Dog Show. I must say he looked impressive when he made that pose, nose in perfect alignment, front right paw raised off the ground and his tail on a perfect plane with his body.

When not on a hunting trip and showing off this grand trick, however, he tended to get himself into a lot of trouble. Like the time one summer evening when he crawled into a drainage pipe beside a neighbor's house down the street. Daddy was working a 3 to 11 p.m. shift when we noticed we hadn't seen Ole Jim for a while. Some of the neighbor kids reported hearing a sad moaning sound from underground next to their garage.

Putting two and two together, we concluded Ole Jim was merely curious about where the pipe led, decided to turn around in mid-adventure, and became stuck in the pipe. Thank goodness, he had sense enough to make some noise.

Mother called Daddy at work, something she only did in dire emergencies. What to do? His answer: "Why, dig up the neighbor's yard, of course. We have to save that valuable dog!"

Well, dozens of volunteers were still digging, now with floodlights, when Daddy arrived just in time to see Ole Jim, happy but muddy, emerging from the bowels of the pipe. The whole neighborhood was clapping and congratulating themselves on a "job well done." It was our neighborhood's "Baby Jessica" moment.

I have no idea what Daddy had to pay to have the pipe replaced, the dirt refilled, and new grass planted in our neighbor's yard. But I never heard him complain about it.

Now Ole Jim was a pretty friendly dog and he thought he was welcome all over town. And in everybody's trash can. One day he came home bloody, dragging one leg behind him. I'm amazed he had the strength to make it home. Daddy was absolutely furious that someone would shoot his magnificent animal. He put Ole Jim in the garage, shut the door tight, and told us to guard the door. He got on his motorcycle and left.

He came back with some bandages, alcohol, and chloroform he had gotten at the local drug store. At least that's what he said. Who knew they sold chloroform at the drugstore? We were not allowed in the garage while Daddy was "operating." After an hour or so, the bullet was removed and Ole Jim was starting to come around.

We were instructed to be super nice to the dog for a few days. And believe me, he loved the attention. He was a slow mover for a while, but was soon back to his old self. All of this seemed perfectly ordinary to us.

One who got even my dad's attention was old Oscar Harmon who lived next door. Oscar and Esther Harmon had moved from Cedartown, Georgia, to Smyrna around the same time we moved onto Adams Drive. They were already pretty old but Oscar was still working.

Now Cedartown, in extreme east Georgia very near the Alabama state line, would make the sleepy communities of Villa Rica, Smyrna, and Cartersville look like Las Vegas. The Harmons were characters who daily amused us. Oscar was stubborn as a mule and Esther followed him around nagging at him. It seemed to work for them.

Oscar turned half his lot into a huge garden in the summer, as most other Southerners did. Except for us. Our yard was full of Daddy's critters. Each night, the Harmons brought over some of the bounty they couldn't eat. About sunset each day, Miz Harmon would take her dishpan to the yard and begin to sprinkle the dirty leftover dishwater on her prize-winning tulips. I never saw a bug go near those tulips.

Neighbors back then were like family. My parents sent us next door each time we had a loose tooth. Miz Harmon tied a string around the

PHYLLIS RICH CARPENTER

tooth, tied the other end of the string to a doorknob, and then slammed the door. She always knew why we were knocking at her back door. One of the Rich girls must need a tooth pulled.

Old Oscar was one of those strange people who could reach his hand up into a beehive to retrieve the honey—without getting a single bee sting. And he loved my dad. He was thrilled when Daddy took him with him on an all-night fishing trip to Lake Allatoona.

Dad came home talking about that trip and went on about it for weeks. Seems they were driving the boat into a little inlet when Daddy spied several snakes dangling from a tree on the bank, directly over where the boat was headed. When Daddy started backing the boat up, old Oscar objected, stood up in the boat and instructed my dad to go forward. He then pulled each snake from the tree limbs and flung them across the water, in a perfectly matter-of-fact-way

The Search - Day 17
Sunday, December 15

River Blasters Push Search for Hunters
Cartersville, Georgia

National Guardsmen set off dynamite Saturday and Sunday in the Etowah River, hoping to bring to the surface the bodies of two duck hunters who have been missing since November 30.

"We blasted every deep hole around the old Indian fish traps," Lt. Col. Horace Clary of Rome, commanding officer of the guardsmen, said.

"There are 15 of those rock traps in 15 miles and we have been blasting in the deep holes near each one."

Col. Clary said that it was the belief of all outdoorsmen familiar with the river that the bodies would be found close to the point where the two men went down. The men, Earl Rich, 35, and Albert O'Shields, 25, of Atlanta, disappeared on a duck-hunting trip November 29.

The boat the men used and a paddle are all that have been found by the searchers.

Col. Clary said that more than 100 volunteers, including 25 or 30 volunteers from the National Guard unit, searched the river Saturday and Sunday. Col. Clary has 11 men on duty for the search.

He said that the unit plans to continue blasting Monday, hoping that the shock waves from the dynamite will bring the hunters' bodies to the surface.

The Atlanta Constitution

Crowds of sightseers and rubberneckers are a daily presence. My aunts have already told the Red Cross that, while we are grateful, none of the coffee and snacks they deliver is aiding the families or searchers. As soon as the truck arrives each day, people come from everywhere. It's as if someone in town tipped them off that the truck was on its way.

At each physical key site of the search, there are sometimes hundreds of people, especially on the weekends. I can't tell the difference between them and the searchers or friends and family members of the O'Shields family, and vice-versa. The strangers don't know any of us.

I'm standing at the riverbank the day the "draggers" round the bend in the river so that they can be seen from our Milam Bridge vantage point. Many of my thirty-plus cousins are there, walking and looking around—so many of us that we are like ants at a picnic. But there is not the usual running, laughing and playing. We know instinctively that it's not the time for merriment.

So how would one know that I am the oldest daughter of one of the missing men? Two old women within my earshot were discussing the search. "Oh," one says, "them boys are nowhere near that water. They've just run off!"

I say nothing, nor do I share this bit of information with my mother. It was not worth mentioning anyway. Foolish old women! Aunt Winnona, who was in high school at the time, remembers a similar experience when a teacher doubted her brother was in the river. Aunt Winnona was not as shy as I was, so she quickly told the teacher, "You don't know my family!"

Two of the O'Shields' brothers, William, twenty, and James, eighteen, had still another experience. They made periodic stops at the store/gas station several miles from the river command sites for gas and provisions.

William relates, "You wouldn't believe the ugly talk about the missing men in that store!" James adds. I spoke up and told them, "That's my brother you're talking about!" Silence followed.

Who knows where such ugliness comes from, but for every person with an ugly comment, there were 200 others with good hearts out there searching day after day in freezing weather.

The old women on the riverbank didn't know what I know. There were three constants in my dad's life: his family (immediate and extended), hunting/fishing, and motorcycles. The last two categories were tied for second place.

One thing I know for sure is that at this time in 1957, my dad is totally in love with baby sister Judy. My mom had been worried that he would be disappointed with another girl. To convince her otherwise, he threw a "welcome home" party for the two of them when she left the hospital.

Me? I was thrilled the baby was a girl, but for the stupidest of reasons. The month before Judy was born, it was Valentine's Day at my school classroom. The teacher had hung paper bags with our names on them up on the bulletin board to accept valentines from our classmates. A boy named Kenneth brought a *huge* box of candy to place in my bag, which promptly tore it loose from the bulletin board and it hit the floor with a large thud.

The teacher made a big deal out of what a sweet gesture Kenneth had made. But I was so shy, the public display had embarrassed me greatly. So you can imagine how I felt when I learned that Daddy planned to name a baby brother, if we had one, "Kenneth."

Somewhere out there is a grown man named Kenneth who has no idea why I broke his heart on Valentine's Day in 1957.

Prior to the party, Daddy rehearsed us to make sure Mother wouldn't get the idea that we were disappointed. But if *he* was disappointed, he sure didn't show it. He was so smitten. To see Daddy each day with our new sister was the sweetest thing. He would come home from work, go straight and pick her up, then play with her for as long as she would tolerate it. He would make faces, funny noises and bounce her on his knees. She would laugh and squeal until she would nearly lose her breath.

Thinking of this on the riverbank made me so sad for the baby. What must she think now that this fabulous creature had disappeared from her daily life? Or that she is bounced around with relatives? My mother's cousin's family had her for weeks in the long run and grew so attached to her, they were heartbroken to give her up in the end.

PHYLLIS RICH CARPENTER

The Search - Day 18
Monday, December 16

Dynamite, Skin Divers Fail To Turn up Bodies
Two Missing Duck Hunters Sought at Etowah's Indian Fish
Traps

Dynamite blasts and skin divers in the Etowah River during the weekend failed to turn up any trace of two duck hunters who have been missing since the last day of November.

National Guardsmen said they let off charges in "every deep hole around the old Indian fish traps" Saturday and Sunday. Lt. Col. Horace Clary of Rome, commanding the unit, said it was thought the bodies of Earl Rich, 35, and Albert O'Shields, 25, might have lodged in the stone traps.

About 100 volunteers, including several men from his National Guard unit, participated in the search Saturday and Sunday, Clary said.

Clary said those familiar with the river believed that if the men drowned, their bodies are near the spot where they went down. Hundreds of searchers have covered a long stretch of the river since the disappearance.

Searchers stretched steel mesh across the Etowah and the flow of water through generators at nearby Allatoona Dam was increased to the maximum in hopes of dislodging the bodies and sweeping the bodies into the nets.

The boat and one paddle used by the hunters have been found but no trace of the men.

The Guard and State Police Sunday had to order motorists away from the search site because heavily jammed traffic was hindering the hunt.

The wives and families of the two men have kept a constant vigil at the riverside for two weeks.

Marietta Daily News

Uncle Esco would try to wade out into the water with his friend, Randy Stone, who was doing some of the dynamiting to try to dislodge anything on the bottom of the river. Uncle Esco said, "I'd walk with him down there. Every time I'd start wading, they'd raise the devil with me to get out. But I'd wade anyhow."

He was limited in the physical search. During WWII, he was assigned to some kind of "administrative" Marine division with duties in the states. He didn't qualify for hazardous duty because, in his wild days, he was in a motorcycle accident that threw him clear as high as a telephone pole. He came down on one leg and limped for the rest of his life.

We were told that the main search was located on one of the river's ancient Indian fish traps. We were not allowed near the site because we were told it was too treacherous to reach. My dad and Albert had not "walked in" but reached the area by boating downstream to it. So it was that we had to speculate what a fish trap might be.

The whole area is a historic site, home to some several thousand Native Americans from AD 1000 to 1550. The explorer Desoto documented their existence in his 1540 expedition of the region. The first Indians in the area were Mississippian Mound Builders, later the Creek Indians. They inhabited the area until driven south by the Cherokees in the eighteenth century.

The first Indians, the Mississippians, built mounds for worship, some of which have been excavated and can be viewed today. They were a society in ritual. Towering over the community, one sixty-three-foot earthen knoll was likely used as a platform for the home of the priest-chief. In another mound, nobility were buried in elaborate costumes accompanied by items they would use in their after-lives.

The V-shaped fish traps the Indians erected in the river were used for catching fish. Who needed rods, reels, hooks, and bait when you could just use stacks of rocks to construct traps? There are at least half a dozen traps in the area of the Etowah where Daddy was hunting and they have survived intact for hundreds of years.

The traps are easily recognizable from the bank or from overhead by the V-shaped rapids, they form. The Indians would place a wicker basket or ramp, like a ski jump, at the end of the "V" and drive the fish downstream by wading and beating the water with sticks. As the fish would try to exit the "V," the additional current would push them up onto the wicker ramp.

20

The Search - Day 21
Thursday, December 19

This night, after the day's unfruitful search, Mother has reached some kind of desperation point. Never had I seen her act that way. But then again, the whole month had been so surreal. Things you couldn't imagine were surrounding us, distorting our view, making "normal" seem as if it had never existed.

Mother has a friend, Betty Sikes, whom she met during her working days at Lockheed. Betty had a new-fangled machine that would dry clothes. She would come and go to our house during the search and clean, folded clothes would magically appear on our beds.

I hear Mother talking to Betty, "I simply can't stand by any longer with him missing day after day. I have to do something! Psychics are *in the Bible*. Maybe one can help us find Earl."

Although we rarely attended church, Mother always said she believed in God. She didn't actually know what the Bible said about psychics, just that they were "in there."

Betty says, "Why didn't you tell me sooner. I know of someone in rural Alabama. We can leave early in the morning."

There would be no way to call in advance, as the psychic had no phone. Nor did she have a TV or newspaper delivery. Betty would get the directions from an acquaintance. She would pick up my mother before daylight. They would return home by late afternoon.

The old woman's house was on a rural dirt road, miles from any other houses, stores, or modern civilization (by 1950s definition). It was a gray clapboard, devoid of any paint, if it ever had any. It was still early morning and both women cautiously approached the front screened porch, which had also seen better days.

Before they could knock, an old man opened the door and said, "Come in. We were expecting you." He explained that he and his wife had spent the night with their son closer to town because of the extreme cold. There was only one small wood-burning stove in the house, which had been built long before the value of insulation was discovered. His wife had awakened her husband in the dark and said, "Someone's coming. We have to go home."

The old woman motioned my mother and her friend to sit at her kitchen table. When Mother started to state her reason for coming, the woman put her finger to her lips to silence my mother. She then took her hands and made a waving motion back and forth. She then spoke the words, "Rolling waters. Rolling waters."

She asked my mother why she wore no jewelry or rings, being as she was most certainly a married woman. My mother had left her rings at home because she was going to a stranger's house in the middle of nowhere. She was afraid of being robbed.

Then the medium proceeded to relate *my mother's whole life story* to her, including events or thoughts that she alone would know. When she got to the part about children, the old woman said that she didn't know if my mother's children were male or female, but that they were all the same sex. She then put up a finger for each child—one, then two fingers in quick succession. Lynn and I are only 18 months apart in age. A third finger went up after a *pause.* Judy was a "surprise baby," born when Lynn was nearly nine and I was 10 ½.

Finally, she stated that she knew my mother had come to inquire about her missing husband. The old woman's most startling information was that she didn't know if he was dead or alive but that he was most certainly *moving.* And that he would be found in three days on an island on which three small streams merged.

Back at the river camp that night as my mother related the story, Uncle Esco had a smile on his face, something I hadn't seen for weeks. He said maybe it was false hope, but at least it was hope. In fact, we were all buoyed by the news. *After all, how could a dead man be moving?*

Uncle Jack was so excited that he made his own quick trip to visit the old woman. He had her draw a map of where to find Daddy. He returned with a map of the small island where Daddy would be found just days later.

The Search - Day 22
Friday, December 20

Hope or no hope, the search goes on. I had been curious about the term "dragging the river" from the start. The very idea of it left a cold, unpleasant feeling in the pit of my stomach.

How does one actually "drag" a river? The official definition is "to pull a grapnel, net, or other device over the bottom of a river, lake, or some other body of water in search of something."

Unofficially, boats line up across the river, almost touching. The men who operate these boats pull grappling hooks until they feel some weight on them. Then they pull up these hooks to see what they've snagged.

I watched them when they approached the Milam Bridge, having already traveled miles downstream from the fish traps. The hooks they would pull up looked like large pitchforks. I was thinking to myself, "If they pull Daddy up at this place while I am watching, I will just die."

The Search - Day 23
Saturday, December 21

Some kind soul has volunteered to ̶
Mother wants us to go shopping with tʰ
These are certainly meant to be funerᵃ

It is easy to use my "big sister influence" to gᵉ⸗ ⸗͵
up. Both she and I protest loudly to our mother and we were prouᵈ ⸗⸗
it. Mother seems to understand and quietly tells us, "They can go back
to the store if we don't need them. But it would be best to have them
just in case."

So we go shopping for the day and it was at least a break from the
cold river. It was strange to be doing normal things again. We got new
wool coats and hats, gloves, dresses with crinolines attached, socks
trimmed in eyelet lace and new patent leather dress shoes. I admit I did
like the shoes.

Unknown to us, my mother had an appointment the same morning.
She was purchasing five cemetery lots at Kennesaw Memorial Park
Cemetery, one for each of us. Her concern was that she and her girls
might all die in a future singular accident. She wanted us all to be buried
next to Daddy.

21

e Hunt

Having somehow lost the lifeline of their boat, Earl and Albert would have to deal with the rising water level with their own ingenuity. Their first move would have been to get to a shoreline with the only question being, "Which one?"

The rocks leading to the north shore are the closest to the men from a proximity standpoint, but they are a longer walk because the rocks cut farther upstream into the river. You would almost be walking straight into the oncoming current and arriving at the bank much farther upstream than you would from the south. If you were to look at the rock formation from above facing upstream, then it would look more like a backwards "check mark" than a V shape, with the north rocks heading upstream and the south rocks curling around towards the shore.

That being said, after exploring the north formations, you really don't have to walk *on* them at all. Oddly enough the water is only about one foot deep in front of the north rocks. Walking is easy on the firm, compacted sand to the north and, compared to the southern route, it takes half the time to cover the required distance to shore. You can actually jog in front of the north rocks!

However, unless you go out there in perfect conditions then you wouldn't know that fact by just observing from the island. Again, the river was higher than usual due to recent rains, so the water would likely have been "stained." The men would not have known this safe route unless they had previously spent a good deal of time at the site.

Uncle Jack later tested both routes and found the south formation nearly impossible to traverse. He said, "I tried to cross the water at the south rocks with the water up to my waist. I had a rope to hold on to. Otherwise, I couldn't have made it because the river was so swift at that point."

He continued, "It swept your feet out from under you. If they had tried to cross at the other side, it would most certainly have been different. The current is simply not as swift over there." The fact that Uncle Jack felt compelled to test both routes suggests that maybe the Rich brothers had not spent a lot of time at the traps—and certainly not during swift current.

Having to make a snap decision, the men chose the south shore as their escape route. The rock formation leading to the south shore does not cut as sharply into the current as does the north formation. It is shorter and gently curls around until it is eventually perpendicular to the current, a *seemingly* quick escape.

In reality, the current is much stronger on the south side due to the river making a slight westward turn. The water is also much deeper in front of the rocks that form the trap. Of course, the two men would not have been trying to walk *in front of* the rocks. They would have been attempting to walk *on top of* the rocks. Rocks in rivers are always slimy and treacherous. The white water effect on the south formation gives you a false sense of confidence that they are indeed rocks conducive to walking on. It even forms a sort of "trail" in the water.

Even if the boat was gone at this point, the south bank offered a more welcoming, larger shore with the train tracks above that would have led them back to Albert's car parked just a mile up river—something that must have crossed their minds after sitting on that island for more than four hours staring at the same scenery. One can easily see how the south formation provided a logical choice for the men in that moment of crisis.

This attempt to traverse the rocks, sadly, was doomed from the start. In order to walk efficiently over rocks in a river, you have to be able to see what you are stepping *towards* and stepping *on*. As they make their desperate push toward the shore, the men are now in waist deep water, which is around thirty-five degrees Fahrenheit, flowing with incredible force and rising exponentially with every passing minute.

According to the *Geotechnical Rock and Water Resources Library*, waist-deep water moving at around seven feet per second would be exerting roughly 294 pounds of lateral force on their hips, legs and feet, which are precariously perched on slippery rocks three feet below the surface.

Standing still is extremely difficult in the current and walking is next to impossible. There is no visibility through the muddy water and each step is a blind one in which the men are praying that their foot will hit something solid below, something that can keep them upright just a little longer and get them one step closer to safety.

Their adrenaline flow, coupled with the roar of the water and the thunder of the freight train passing on the tracks above them is creating a surreal-like situation in their heads. To make matters worse, after at least three or four minutes in the freezing water, they are losing feeling in their legs and feet. Their water-filled boots and heavily soaked clothing are working in tandem against them, squeezing their bodies, and taxing their strength.

Even their precious guns are a liability now. Nothing at this point is working in their favor and there is no way that they can do anything to help one another. Each man is locked in his own personal life and death struggle. They fight valiantly with every ounce of strength to keep hold of the rocks as the unrelenting force of the water fights in return to dislodge them.

The rising water eventually swept away the boat itself, the inanimate object that delivered them to the island. The south shore, where the rock formation reaches land below the railroad tracks, is a rocky beach, so the boat likely was never tied up at all if indeed that is where it sat that morning. Tying it up would not have been necessary and it probably was sitting there on the rocks as the water began to rise. The men likely planned on walking over to it at the end of their hunt and launching it below the traps to carry them back down to Milam Bridge and Earl's truck.

Its discovery miles downstream below Hardin Bridge, along with a paddle, led people to believe that the rising water swamped the two men and that the boat had capsized. The general consensus was: two men in boat on a river + water release + two missing men = capsized boat. But there is a great possibility that the boat had capsized on its own without Earl and Albert. It likely drifted downstream, possibly for miles before becoming entangled in trees or brush, eventually flipping over from the unrelenting force of the rising water. It was one of few clues, a finger pointing in the wrong direction.

In the end, there is no reaching the bank or even coming close to reaching the bank. Once footing is inevitably lost and the unforgiving current finally takes hold of them, their upper bodies (the last remnants of hope and warmth in their epic battle) are plunged into the freezing water, literally taking their breath away in the process.

The water just below the south rock formation is at least six feet deep when the water is at its lowest. Trying to "push off" with their feet is impossible, as the water was just too deep. Their natural instinct as hunters is to hold onto their guns, even if it means paddling with feet and only one hand.

Each man struggles to stay above water, abandoning his gun in a last desperate attempt to swim to shore. They reach for dead trees, rocks or anything to grab hold of, but it's a lost effort. There was, simply put, absolutely no chance of escape as the men were swept away downriver and *into eternity.*

22

The Search – Day 24
Sunday, December 22

During my night's sleep, something stripped me of all hope that my dad was alive. All I know is that when I went to bed, I was certain my dad was alive and would come home to us. But the moment my eyes opened this morning, I was positive that he was dead. And no information to the contrary would make me believe any different. It was like passing through a heavy curtain with no way back. This was information I felt my mother needed to know at once.

It was still very early. In the kitchen, Mother was in her usual place at the table drinking her coffee and smoking her cigarette. The friends, relatives, and neighbors would arrive in a short while and we would head for the river. She was accustomed to me being up early and coming in to check on her. But on this morning, I simply said in a very calm voice, "Mother, Daddy's dead."

I'll never forget the look on her face. She slowly put her coffee down, turned her head to me, and looked at me like she thought I was crazy. She didn't say one word.

And when Uncle Jack came to our house late that night after the day's search, I knew exactly why he had come.

Mama Rich and Winona were still at the river when Daddy was found, but just barely. Their ride was already driving off with them when Aunt Elaine's husband Herbert runs up to their car window and says, "They've found Pinky!"

We had already left for the day. We were home, fed, bathed and in our pajamas. Lynn and I were on the sofa playing with paper dolls. I heard a car door shut out front. Mother said, "Who could that be this late?" My hands froze with the paper doll in them. I stared blankly at the doll. Lynn played on as if nothing was unusual. I didn't know who was in the car, but I absolutely knew why they were there.

Uncle Jack came in, said softly to Mother, "We found Earl."

She turned to go from the kitchen to her bedroom, I assume to get dressed, then turned back to him and said, "Is he dead?" Uncle Jack simply nodded, yes. Mother cried quietly as she rounded the corner to her bedroom. She didn't even look over at us.

We got dressed, too and went to a funeral home in Cartersville. By the time we got there, it was after midnight. I hated the smell of the place. And that even though our dad had been found, we still had to just take people's word for it. He wouldn't be coming home with us. Not now. Not ever.

Jack was like Daddy, quiet and happy to just blend into the background of a crowd. As if they could. Strong people always stand out. Some forty years after he found my dad's body, on the little island where "three small streams merged," he was very soft-spoken when talking to me about it. He looked down the entire time, probably picturing the actual event. He said:

> You know I found Earl. I knew it was him. He was face down. His jacket was pulled up over his head. I recognized his boots. Me and Gilford Taylor found him. We'd been searching for Earl so long. We did things to pass the time. Gilford and I had been shooting squirrels as we drifted along. And there was Earl at an island. Gilford looked at me and said, "You all right, Jack? You all right?"
>
> We didn't touch him. We left him there because he wasn't going nowhere. And the law had to be there in case there was any foul play. I told the Civil Defense to keep it quiet since I wanted to tell Pat, your mother, myself. I still remember Pat by her dresser crying. I was crying, too.

I still miss Earl. I thought the world of him. He didn't beat around the bush. My brothers were real different. Esco will walk in circles when he talks to you, but Earl would tell you the truth outright. He told it just like it is.

The Search - Day 25
Monday, December 23

Body of Smyrna Hunter Found In Etowah River
Search Is Continued For Second Victim of November Boat
Mishap

The search was over today for one of two duck hunters missing since November 29 on the Etowah River.

The victim's brother and another searcher found the partly-submerged body of Earl Rich, 35, of Smyrna, at an island about six miles downriver from where he and Albert O'Shields, of Atlanta, began their hunting trip last month.

Jack Rich and Gilford Taylor were going up the river in a boat searching the banks when they came to the island. Deciding to circle the island, the pair spotted an object in the water and upon investigation, found that the object was Rich's body.

The pair proceeded downstream for a mile to where a steel net has been stretched across the river. In order not to disclose the discovery to hundreds of spectators on the bank, Rich and Taylor slowly searched along the net, and then went to the bank to talk with other searchers.

Rich then sought out Captain McKelvey of the National Guard and told him of their discovery. A small party quietly left for the island and recovered the victim's fully clothed body.

Searchers said the body apparently had washed up on the island during high water and was left when the water receded.

Members of the Rich family have kept a vigil on the river bank during the search, in which the National Guard and hundreds of volunteers have participated.

PHYLLIS RICH CARPENTER

Rich was a veteran of six years in the Navy. He attended Marietta public schools. He and O'Shields were employees of Atlantic Steel Company of Atlanta, which has helped finance search operations.

Funeral services for Rich were held at 4 p.m. today in Olive Springs Baptist Church. Officiating were the Rev. H. B. Deakins, the Rev. Franklin Rogers and the Rev. Frank Bradley. Burial was at Kennesaw Memorial Park Cemetery. Dobbins Funeral Home was in charge.

Survivors include his wife, Mrs. Patricia Reed Rich; three daughters, Phyllis Rich, Lynn Rich, and Judith Rich; the mother, Mrs. Homer R. Rich, Marietta; three brothers, Esco, Jack, and Harold Rich; seven sisters, Edith Pearson, Ruth Ray, Elaine Mitchell, Winnona Rich, Rheba Hamilton, Dorothy King, and Athaleen Garner.

Marietta Daily Journal

Esco said he told Jack he would be the one to find his brother, but Jack argued with him about it. He did not want to be *the one*. He and Taylor, my dad's good friend from Atlantic Steel, made one last run up the river in their boat that evening. They decided to circle around a little island when they saw something sticking up in the water. All Jack said was, "There's Earl."

They didn't want to arouse suspicion back at the steel mesh command site because of all the bystanders. They got out of the boat and went slowly in to the tent of the National Guard sergeant. Jack told them they'd found Earl and the Guard sent a boat back up after him.

The Funeral

Three gorgeous sisters owned their own hair salon in our little town of Smyrna, Georgia. It was called Leila's Beauty Salon. Unknown to Lynn and I, they had volunteered to do our hair and our mother's hair on the day of the funeral.

They would open up early so that we were the only ones in the shop. It was our town's "Truvie's" as in *Steel Magnolias*. Only on that morning, there was no laughter or fun. Lynn and I said nothing and the salon sisters didn't bother us with trivial conversation. It was a sad event to be followed by other sad events of the day.

By 10:00 a.m., our large, extended family met first at Dobbins Funeral Home in Marietta, up the road from Smyrna. My mother, Lynn and I, one grandfather, two grandmothers and ten uncles and aunts were gathered into a small front room. We barely fit along with my father's casket.

It would be the first time we had seen the casket. Lynn wanted to see inside but an aunt or uncle told her to remember him as he was in life. Actually, it wasn't possible to see inside. My mother had had to pay extra for a specialized "sealable" casket due to the decomposition of my father's body.

Someone came in and said they needed to move his casket to the hearse. It was eerily quiet until the moment they laid hands on the casket. Suddenly, Aunt Rheba let out a scream. It was like the little Dutch guy unplugging the hole in the dam. Everyone in the room fell apart. I have never heard such painful wailing—before or since.

The little white church was already filled when we reached it, with standing room only, the front rows reserved for family. We began our long walk down the center aisle to the sound of sad music. I could feel my heart pounding.

My mother, who still looked like a teenager, had become a twenty-nine-year-old widow, broken-hearted and barely holding herself together. Lynn and I walked alongside her in our "just in case" clothes and our "Leila's Beauty Salon hairdos." I can't even imagine how sad it was for these hundreds of people to see us walking down that aisle. It was something so unnatural, so out of place, so unthinkable.

In front of the flag-draped casket was a special flower arrangement my mother had ordered to be from all of us. There were four interlocking hearts of red roses, graduating in size. Each heart represented one of us, with the tiniest heart at the bottom representing baby Judy. Judy's heart was covered with little rosebuds instead of opened roses.

Lynn complained about her hat all day, tugging at it nonstop. But constant in my mother's life was that we all be appropriately dressed for any occasion in life. So the hat stayed on. There was never a question about that.

Lynn squirmed throughout the service and looked around as if to ask, "What in the world are we doing here?" Her complete denial mindset was still intact, but I was trapped in a grown-up world of reality. I was now eleven-by-*two*-months, and it seemed as if my childhood had been over forever—although it ended just the month before.

On everyone's mind was how could such a thing happen to someone so young, so full of life? It was two days before Christmas. I remember clearly what one of the preachers said. He gave what he thought would be a comforting explanation, that God wanted another gift under his tree in heaven.

I wasn't comforted. It would be years before God and I would be friends again.

As we left the church, someone came up to us and handed us a large envelope. Inside was a snapshot taken at a family reunion a few months earlier. The black and white photo had been thoughtfully blown up into an 8 x 10 portrait of us. Daddy was holding the baby. Both Daddy and I were squinting from the sun in our eyes. Then and forever, it would be the only family portrait with the five of us that we would ever possess. And it would be a long time before I could bear to look at it.

As we walked to the cars for the drive to the cemetery, I heard someone whisper, *"They found Albert O'Shields."*

Our long caravan made its way to the cemetery. Another crowd was gathered by the graveside in addition to those coming from the church. It was a sunny but freezing day. The sky was beautiful. The seven military personnel in their dress uniforms were already at attention for the twenty-one-gun salute. I recall that one of the seven was an African-American.

Now this was the beginning of a time of crisis and change in the South, namely segregation vs. integration. There wasn't much mention of it in our household. My father had been in the Navy and traveled the whole country and the world, so likely his thinking had been broadened from his Georgia farm upbringing.

These graveyard sites made me think of Daddy's black friend, Leonard. Leonard, a constant visitor to Daddy's backyard motorcycle shop, mostly wanted free advice about his bike. So he would pick my father's brain. And sometimes my Dad would just go ahead and fix Leonard's motorcycle for free, saying he had an old part he didn't need anyway. And I could hear him and Leonard laughing outside our house. Sometimes Daddy would laugh about Leonard even after he had left the house. I looked for Leonard in the burial crowd but there were too many people. I wondered what Leonard would do now without his good friend Earl.

On December 23, 1957, the day of my father's funeral, I was so moved by all seven of the military personnel who had come out on that cold day to honor my father.

All I remember apart from that is someone handing my mother the neatly folded American flag, which had been atop my father's casket and the sound of the twenty-one-gun-salute. We had been around guns all our lives, but the sound of the seven guns in unison was more like a cannon going off. I covered my ears. Lynn, fidgeting on the edge of her chair, nearly fell off.

The saddest day of my life had not yet ended. Mother would take us with her to an Atlanta funeral home that evening for Albert O'Shield's visitation. When we returned home, representatives from Atlantic Steel Company brought food and gifts to our house. One gift was the new TV, which my dad had promised us for Christmas. The men seemed so happy to hear our squeals of delight.

But for our family, Christmas would never be the same. A few years later, my dad's sister, Ruth (the other redhead), would die of a heart attack on the way to a hospital on this holiday. Cousin Sandra would say, "It made Christmas very hard for a long time."

23

BULLETIN: The body of Albert O'Shields was found this morning at 10:35 just below the old Indian fish traps where the hunters were last seen by a train crew in water waist deep, holding their guns above their heads.

O'Shields' body was found about four and one-half miles up the river from the spot were Rich was found Sunday about 5 p.m. Warrant Officer H. B. Richards of the National Guard and three men from Calhoun were in the boat that dragged the body of O'Shields from the bottom, where it was imbedded in the mud.

Marietta Daily Journal

Claude O'Shields, Albert's father, and his brother William had been at the river constantly from the beginning. William would occasionally operate one of the boats assigned to check out objects, which would be caught in the mesh net across the river. They were visible from the shore because of the ripples or wave pattern changes near the fence.

Once, William dipped his hand into the water to feel for the object that was lodged. He felt "hair" and was horrified, as he silently prayed, "Please don't be my brother!" Thank God, it turned out to be the silky end of a sheath or corn.

After a few days of initial leave, Robert O'Shields, second born behind Albert, had to return to his active duty position in Texas with the US Navy. But James O'Shields, 18 and in Army basic training, had been given a second emergency leave, and as fate would have it, was on the Etowah when his brother Albert was found. He and his brother William were in a boat digging in the water with sticks. James says, "We didn't even know what we were doing. We were just digging."

On shore, their father had just been notified of the discovery of Albert's body. He approached James and William and motioned to them to pull into shore. There he said simply and softly, "Let's go home, boys. Let's go home."

Albert was found lying on his back as if he were sleeping. His knee was exposed by the lowered water level. One foot was up under a rock, a factor that may have prevented his body from surfacing as my dad's had. It may have been that the water-generating authorities were not convinced the men were actually in the water. Thus, they continued to release large amounts of water the entire month.

After my father's body was found, they lowered the river considerably, a factor that aided in finding Albert. His father Claude would be bitter for a long time about the water levels. Even after the recoveries, it was his strong stand that it should never have taken nearly a month to recover his son.

Robert, back on naval duty in Texas, was unable to return home for Albert's funeral. Funerals for drowning victims who are badly decomposed must be conducted quickly. Both my dad and Albert were buried early the next day following their recoveries.

Body of Second Hunter Is Lifted from Etowah
Cartersville, Georgia
December 23

> The body of the second missing duck hunter was recovered from the Etowah River today less than 24 hours after discovery of his companion's body.
>
> National Guardsmen reported they located the body of Albert O'Shields, twenty-five, of Atlanta, just below some old Indian rock fish traps where a train crew reported seeing the men shortly after the start of a duck-hunting trip Nov. 29.
>
> His brother, Jack Rich of Austell, and a close friend, Gilford Taylor of Marietta, who were patrolling the river in a boat, found the body of Earl Rich, thirty-five, of Smyrna, yesterday afternoon.

Rich's body was about five miles downstream from the spot where guardsmen located the body of O'Shields with drag hooks.

Relatives, National Guardsmen from the Rome unit and employees of the Atlantic Steel Co. in Atlanta, where the two men worked, all took part in the lengthy search.

Funeral services for Mr. O'Shields will be at 3:30 p.m. Tuesday in Westview Abbey Chapel. The Rev. R.D. Walker and the Rev. Chester Vaughn will officiate. Burial will be in Westview Cemetery.

Surviving are his wife, the former Elaine Bullard of Lyerly; his parents, Mr. and Mrs. C.E. O'Shields; a sister, Mrs. David Keller and five brothers, William, James, John and Carl O'Shields, all of Atlanta; Robert O'Shields, Orange, Tex. and his grandmother, Mrs. Martha Hoy, New York City.

Atlanta Journal

A few years before Albert's death, a new cemetery, Westview, had been built near the O'Shields home in Atlanta. Salesmen for the cemetery had canvassed the neighborhood with special discount offers. Ellen O'Shields, along with many of her neighbors, purchased lots. Ellen paid $400 for four spaces but never dreamed she would need them so soon or for such a sad occurrence. She had been paying $10 per month on the debt for the lots.

James was at the funeral home when his brother's body was brought in. Aside from Elaine O'Shields, no one knows for sure if anyone else viewed the body, but it is believed that Albert's father, Claude, was asked to identify it.

James stood outside the room where his brother's body was being cared for. He was close enough to hear the plastic bag that contained his brother's body being lowered into the casket—a sound that cut him to the core.

A cousin in the O'Shields family, Melissa, was also eleven years old in 1957. She remembers being told she could open one of her Christmas presents early. It was a dress to wear to Albert's funeral.

PHYLLIS RICH CARPENTER

Albert had many friends and they were gathered together on this day, along with the family. Albert's brothers can remember wondering how their modest family was able to rent the Abbey Chapel at Westview Cemetery, which is very majestic. The family entered through a side door to the packed facility. They recall that the song played was "Beyond the Sunset."

None of the brothers had ever seen a casket being lowered into the ground before Albert's. A mere walk through a cemetery seeing markers and tombstones and flowers cannot convey the horror of seeing a loved one being lowered into the cold, dark ground, especially when the deceased is so young.

Later, when James was back at basic training, someone was reading a newspaper with a news story and pictures of the search. Seeing James' last name on his uniform, he asked James if that was his family. James broke completely down. Not long after that, another man approached him to ask if Albert O'Shields was his brother.

When James nodded yes, the man said, "I'm one of the men who found your brother."

It's a small world. And when your family tragedy has been in the newspapers for a month, everybody knows your name.

Albert's friend Ed Townsend, from high school and the Navy, called home in 1957 and learned about the search for Albert. He remembers, "I was shocked. He was athletic and a strong swimmer. The Navy taught us how to survive in water. Why, we had to tread water for at least an hour in boot camp!"

After the two funerals, our two families, who were not acquainted before the drowning, went our separate ways. *It would be more than 55 years before any one of us would meet again!* But we would continue to live in parallel worlds.

24

When we reached the Atlanta funeral home that night for visitation with the O'Shields' family, it was reminiscent of the scene of my own father's homecoming—hundreds of people, hushed whispers. It was not like saying goodbye to someone who lived a long and happy life—just a "this is all wrong" atmosphere.

Moments later, Elaine O'Shields greeted us. She and my mother embraced for the longest time without talking. Elaine O'Shields was younger but much taller than my mother was. Their uneven embrace was like watching my mother and my much-taller father embrace. On every other occasion that I had seen Elaine, she was crying and distraught. Now, oddly, she seemed sad, yes, but composed and strong—as if a sense of relief had swept over her. She had finally found her husband and could bury him.

My mother quietly asked Elaine, "Did you see Albert?" I think my mother was still troubled that she had been discouraged from viewing my father's body. Elaine said she had. Mother looked directly down at me.

At that moment, I realized that she was aware that I rarely left her side and that I hung on every bit of information she received. She didn't share information directly with Lynn or me. It had to be "gathered" by eavesdropping. But this night, she looked down at me and said, "Stay right here." Then she and Elaine entered a private room and shut the door.

When my mother emerged, she was visibly shaken and crying. I didn't ask at that time, but later I asked her what Elaine had told her. My mother simply shook her head "no." She never disclosed those details to me, carrying them with her to her death in 1994.

Through the years, I still needed to know about my father's body, even as my mother had when she spoke to Elaine O'Shields. I only knew about the expensive casket that had to be modified to fit my father's bloated body, the satin lining and pillow removed, a special "seal" not contained on most caskets.

Now that information is readily available on the Internet in graphic detail. It is not for the faint-hearted. As drownings go, you can't do worse than to drown in a river. Moving water makes it difficult for recovery, as does underwater obstruction like timber or brush. If a body sinks to a deep pocket, it quickly covers with silt.

When people sink below the surface of the water, they initially hold their breath as long as they can, then involuntarily inhale a large volume of water. In most instances, this water enters the lungs. In other cases, the water reaches the larynx causing a spasm that results in "dry drowning."

In both cases, the gasping for air may continue for several minutes until breathing ceases. Organs and tissues are deprived of oxygen until the situation becomes irreversible and death occurs. The point at which a person dies depends largely on the age of the victim and the temperature of the water, but usually somewhere between three and ten minutes. Most often people lose consciousness within three minutes of slipping below the water.

The human body weighs slightly more than fresh water. So when individuals become unconscious, they sink. And generally, a drowning victim will reach the bottom of a body of water in spite of the depth, unless it meets some obstruction on the way down. As the body descends further, the pressure of the water compresses gasses in the abdomen wall and chest cavities. As a result, the body becomes heavier the further down it goes until it reaches the bottom.

Almost without exception, a body lying on the bottom of a river eventually will surface because of the gas formed in its tissues as a result of decay and the action of internal bacteria. Witnesses to this event have described bodies breaking the surface of the water with great force, like the popping of a cork. So those searching for my father and his friend made a constant up and down search each day by boat, not knowing when, where, or if a body would be spotted, where there was none the day before.

In some cases, the body may remain immersed. Extremely deep, cold water conditions may prevent a corpse from ever becoming buoyant enough to overcome the immense water pressure. Though not voiced out loud in front of me, this fear was pervasive in the minds of my mother and other relatives. Although one can walk or wade across some parts of the Etowah in non-generating times, there are also deep areas in the river.

Victims are usually found on the bottom relatively close to the drowning site. We had a good idea of this site because my dad had duplicated this duck-hunting trip a number of times with his brother, Esco. They would put the boat in at Hwy. 61 bridge near Ladds just south of Cartersville, float down to Brown's fish traps, then, after a fun day of duck hunting, take the boat down to Milam Bridge to exit.

So those were the beginning and ending points in the search, with the steel net placed across the river by Atlantic Steel Company at Hardin Bridge, some miles below Milam Bridge, a fail-safe measure in case the bodies somehow slipped past the searchers.

The "wild card" in this scenario was the generating waters, which created flash flood situations that could make deep river pockets even deeper and currents stronger. So a victim's body, rather than being found close to the site of death, could roll on the bottom for a distance. Or, if it floated to the surface, it could drift in the current before washing ashore or coming to rest in a back eddy. And this is exactly what happened in the case of my father's body.

There was no autopsy performed on my dad or Albert O'Shields. The state of their bodies would likely not have yielded any pertinent evidence apart from the visual inspection of the bodies. Autopsies on drowning victims are not an exact science. Since in some percentage of drowning victims, there is no water present in the lungs, investigators often make a drowning diagnosis only with a knowledge of the circumstances and exclusion of other causes.

PHYLLIS RICH CARPENTER

Could the person swim well? What was the individual doing at the time? Did anyone witness the incident? What was the likely time of death? If any injuries exist on the body, were they caused before, during, or after death?

The latter question is problematic since my father's body likely met with resistance as it traveled downstream. We already knew how long my father and Albert had been in the water, so time of death was not an issue.

Uncle Jack would never speak of my dad's body, beyond the small statement he gave me before his own death. Uncle Harold said it's best to "leave it be." Uncle Esco was not allowed to see his brother's body, so he had no first-hand information.

My cousin Tommy coincidentally was at the bank when the boat came back containing my father's body. What he saw saddened him for the rest of his life. All my cousins adored my dad—especially the boys because they had often hunted and fished with him. Tommy gave me the one solid piece of information in that he said fish and turtles had done their damage. Marine life often does damage to a body, whether animal or human.

Water differences and climatic conditions have an effect on the decomposition of the body. Generally, cold and swiftly moving water preserve bodies, whereas heavy clothing and warmer water hasten decomposition. My father and Albert were wearing heaving clothing, boots, and hunting jackets, whose pockets were likely loaded with heavy shotgun shells.

Had either man been found at the drowning site and *much earlier on*, likely their arms would have been bent toward their faces. It appears that drowning victims try to cover their mouths to prevent drowning. Often, they clinch their fists. Sometimes objects may be found in their hands as they groped for any means of rescue—even soil or gravel from the bottom.

When Uncle Jack said he knew he had found Earl *because he recognized his boots*, it is a very telling statement. The conditions my father and Albert O'Shields were exposed to would have made victim identification difficult. In any event, I am certain that my father would have never wanted his own brother to find him in such a state. And my uncles made the right decision to discourage my mother from viewing her beloved husband's body.

The reality of the appearance of a drowning victim is shocking. We all know that the skin on our hands and feet will wrinkle from a long bath or hours in a pool. But for a drowning victim, the outer layer of skin may become completely separated from the feet and hands.

Before he returned to the Army, James O'Shields was asked to stay with Elaine a few nights at the apartment she had shared with her husband, Albert. She had asked for Albert's hunting boots and jacket. After a time, she asked James to take them away. The sight of them was more than she could bear.

James took his brother's clothes and shoes and buried them. He says Elaine could not know how hard that was for him. He recalls, with sadness, that there was flesh still in the boots.

Like Elaine O'Shields, my mother was given the option of having my father's jacket and boots. So one evening soon after the funeral, someone brought his caked-in-mud jacket and boots to us. She kept them in a little closet on the back porch that Daddy built—until she learned that the presence of them was upsetting to me. I couldn't sleep knowing that they were there, just a few steps from my bed. Soon after, they disappeared.

These victims were not strangers to us, but precious loved ones. So these clinical details cut into our hearts. At very tender ages, we had learned of or were exposed to things no one should ever have to see or hear.

PHYLLIS RICH CARPENTER

25

Tuesday, December 24

Many Hours Searching; Costly Operations Led To Recovery of Bodies

Ending an intensive round-the-clock search lasting twenty-four days by members of the National Guard unit from Rome under direction of Captain F. I. McKelvey, the body of Albert O'Shields, twenty-six, of Atlanta was pulled from a V-shaped rock ledge submerged in the Etowah River.

The Daily Tribune News
Cartersville, Georgia

Families in this modern time would find many more resources available in the search for their loved ones due to advances in technology. Side-scan sonar, for example, has resulted in the recovery of victims that otherwise may have remained missing without refloating to the surface.

Drowning is the third leading cause of accidental death, according to the World Health Organization, with an estimated nearly four hundred thousand deaths annually worldwide. The global burden of death from drowning is found in all economies and regions. So likely just about everyone has had an acquaintance or relative drown.

Weekly, we read in our local newspapers of drowning deaths in our respective areas. Occasionally, there is a drowning of a well-known figure, such as the actress Natalie Wood. Questions persist for years about such tragedies.

A drowning is extremely hard on families—with "closure," as it is called now, being almost unattainable. And the families will hold vigil as long as needed in order to bring home their loved one. Quite often, a family member finds the drowning victim. We, of course, were determined to find the bodies of our missing loved ones in 1957. However, the word "closure" was not a term we used then. But if I were to define closure, it would be this:

> Closure is when your missing loved one is located safe and sound and returns to home and family.

If Daddy and Albert had managed to get out of the river that day, though they may have lost their guns and other belongings, Daddy would have laughed and made light of his latest adventure. He would have come through the door with The Grin, saying, "Guess what happened to me today!"

It would have been just another great true story, which, up to then, defined our lives. Absent that safe and happy return, though, there would be no closure. All one can do is move forward. Actually, you move forward even against your will. The earth is spinning and you spin with it.

You receive a life sentence of learning to live with a broken heart. When I pass people on the street, I wonder how many people I pass have learned to do just that. Lynn and I were urged to "move on," but neither of us wanted to. We wanted to stay behind. We would much rather have stayed on an eternal river search than to have been made to live life without our beloved father.

Some said he would have wanted us to move on. That made no sense to me. I believe I can say with a certainty what my dad would have wanted. *He just wanted to come home.*

My mother would place a personal ad in the *Atlanta Journal-Constitution* the month following my father's funeral:

CARD OF THANKS

It is the desire of the family of Earl R. Rich to thank the people of Atlanta, Fulton County and surrounding areas for the efforts put forth to recover the body of our beloved following the tragedy which took his life on Nov. 29, 1957. We are indeed grateful for the time, material, money, and gifts provided during those heartbreaking days before and after he was found.

The Family of Earl R. Rich.

After the burial of his son, Claude O'Shields would visit the Governor's office again—this time to offer his thanks. Marvin Griffin would write back:

Dear Mr. O'Shields:

I am so sorry that I was absent from the office Thursday when you came by to express your appreciation to me for our help during your recent tragedy.

The little contribution that we made to you in your hour of sorrow was certainly not in proportion to our sympathetic feeling for you in your bereavement.

Mrs. Griffin joins me in expressing our deepest sympathy to you and the family.

Sincerely,

Marvin Griffin
Governor, State of Georgia

History really does repeat itself. The danger that bodies of water pose are not a new phenomenon. It is almost a certainty that some ancient peoples lost their lives in those waters they depended upon—whose secrets we will never know. Only in the last hundred years or so have we come to know the personal accounts of drowning victims in and around our areas. When they finally began to be documented, they yielded amazing details:

Death in the River
Cartersville, Georgia
October 17, 1889

Mr. Miles Arnold meets a horrible death yesterday. While starting to cross the Etowah River, he falls overboard and his lifeless body is found in the stream.

Mr. Miles Arnold, a prominent farmer and citizen of the seventeenth district, met his death yesterday by drowning in the Etowah River.

Mr. Arnold was postmaster at Ford and every Wednesday and Saturday, carries the mail between that place and Kingston. Yesterday morning he left as usual with the mail, expecting to come down to Cartersville on the morning train, returning on the afternoon train to Kingston, and return with the mail.

But he never reached Kingston. His family waited for his arrival home last night, but they waited in vain. When long after his usual time has passed, they grew uneasy. A searching party was made up and started off on the road Mr. Arnold had taken. When they reached the Etowah River about half a mile from home, a horrible sight met their gaze. In the river, not far from the bank and in shallow water, the small, flat-bottomed boat used for crossing was found turned upside down. Under it was the lifeless body of Mr. Arnold.

It is supposed that Mr. Arnold was bailing the water out of the boat, preparatory to crossing the stream. He is subject to attacks of vertigo and at this time one of the attacks came on him, he staggered and fell into the rushing water below, capsizing the boat as he went down.

The horrified and grief-stricken searchers, as quickly as possible, put him in a buggy and carried him to the home he had left that morning in such fine spirits.

What a difference of feeling in that household of morning and night. Truly, the bright, glad sunshine had been exchanged for gloomy darkness.

Mr. Arnold is a gentleman of sixty-two years of age and leaves a large family of grown children, nine in number. Last year, he lost one of his arms in his gin and this fact perhaps prevented him from making a greater effort to save his life.

The Cartersville Express

PHYLLIS RICH CARPENTER

Death in the Etowah
Jack Griffin Charged With Drowning Old Man Noah Blakely
Cartersville, Georgia
December 3, 1896

Last Friday night a party of five Negroes were crossing the Etowah River in a small boat, which was capsized about the middle of the stream, and all were thrown out. Four of them managed to reach the shore, but Noah Blakely, who was an old man, was drowned. The other Negroes left him to his fate and did not try to render assistance.

Among the party was a Negro from Chattanooga named Jack Griffin. He was chiefly instrumental in capsizing the boat and it is thought that his purpose was to get rid of Noah Blakely, who was one of the eyewitnesses in the murder of Greene Smith by William Jones, who was arrested in Chattanooga last week.

At the investigation by the coroner's jury, the evidence against Jack Griffin was thought to be sufficient and he was bound over to court upon the charge of murdering Noah Blakely and is now in jail to wait the January term.

The Courant American
Cartersville, Georgia

And in November and December 1957, my father's drowning and Albert O'Shields' became a historical record.

As it turns out, we had another missing family member long before I was born. Cousin Leon found this information in an old census after hearing his mother, Aunt Edith, and Uncle Esco speak about it for years. Seems an old uncle, "Doc" (Benjamin Franklin Marlow), had moved out to Wyoming and had a ranch. He and some of his ranch hands had gone out to round up some horses or cattle.

His seven-year-old daughter, Alice Eloise Marlow, followed him. He sent her back home. A blizzard came up and she lost her way and froze to death. They found her body the next day, pretty close to the house. Her mother died within the month, some said of a "broken heart." I knew just how she felt.

The O'Shields family also had its own missing relative from the past, and the similarities to the 1957 tragedy are uncanny. Claude O'Shields' second cousin, twice-removed—also coincidentally named Albert—was known for his fast living and troubles with the law. He lived in Columbus, Georgia, around the early 1930s.

He was a bit of a "river rat" known to run trotlines on the Chattahoochee River, which runs right through Columbus. Jobs were hard to come by in that era, so selling the fish would bring in a little money.

A trotline is a heavy fishing line with baited hooks attached at intervals by means of branch lines called snoods. A snood is a short length of line, which is attached to the main line using a clip or swivel, with the hook at the other end. A trotline can be set so that it covers the width of a channel, river, or stream with baited hooks and can be left unattended. They are now illegal in many states.

This particular Albert had two favorite pastimes: playing the fiddle and harmonica, and fishing on the Chattahoochee from his sixteen-foot flat-bottomed Cyprus bateau. One cold day in February 1935, Albert, dressed in a blue serge suit for warmth, put on his overalls over the suit, tied his size 7 ½ shoes, paddled his bateau out into the swift Chattahoochee current, and ran his trot lines for the last time.

The following article appeared in the Alabama newspaper *Opelika Daily News* on Monday, March 11, 1935:

BODY FOUND IN RIVER THAT OF COLUMBUS MAN
Was Found Saturday, Been Missing Since Xmas

The body of a white man found Saturday evening in the Chattahoochee River near Bartlett's Ferry was today identified as that of Albert O'Shields of 337 28th Street, Columbus, Georgia, Sheriff Emmett Holt reported. O'Shields' son, Charles Benjamin O'Shields, from contents found in the man's pockets, identified the body. It was said he had been missing since Christmas.

PHYLLIS RICH CARPENTER

Sheriff Holt, Coroner Paul McGinty, and Harris County, Georgia officers and coroner were called late Saturday when the body was found in the main channel of the river about 2 miles from Bartlett's Ferry and about 10 miles from Columbus. Coroner McGinty said the body had become hung on some bushes near the bank and was discovered by Cal Ray, who was fishing there, about 4:40 Saturday afternoon.

Lee County and Harris County officials were notified and at once began an investigation. The body was recognized as that of a white man but could not be identified as the coroner said it had been in the water at least 3 weeks.

Today the body was identified as that of O'Shields, about 50 years old, of Columbus. It was said O'Shields was a fisherman and often went off by himself to camp and fish. Officers said his son told them he had gone off about Christmas to camp on a creek in Harris County and had not been heard from since.

No foul play was suspected as no evidence of such could be found on the body. It was believed possible that the man might have fallen into the water and drowned. Coroner McGinty returned a verdict of "death by causes unknown."

When found, the body was clothed in heavy underwear, shirt, and blue serge suit. In the pockets of the suit, officers found two pocketknives, a bunch of keys and a cigarette case with the name of a Columbus firm stamped on it. O'Shields' son identified him by one of the keys found in his pockets, officers said.

The man was described as about 5 feet 9 inches tall, weighing around 150 pounds and with good teeth.

His wife and son survive him.

The family, however, always believed that Albert's death was the result of foul play. He had recently had an argument with some moonshiners operating nearby, as well as a run-in with the Columbus Police. There are questions which have gone unanswered. Just as in our 1957 tragedy, *rivers keep secrets,* so the truth will never be known.

26

Whether we liked it or not, we were now forced to make a new life for ourselves. Over the next six months, the possessions my dad loved would sadly leave, one at a time: his truck, motorcycles and tools, and parts out of his garage. He had quite an inventory.

We would still hear the roar of a motorcycle riding up, which was like a knife sticking into our hearts. Only it would be an old friend or acquaintance of Daddy's who had heard through the grapevine that "Pinky's" stuff was available for sale.

Of course, Mother didn't know what they were worth. She would just ask for a "contribution." I like to think these men gave her more than the objects were worth. They looked so sad to be going through a dead man's personal treasures. And sad for the girls he had left behind.

Everywhere there was sadness and stillness. Daddy's vineyard, trees, and plants were unkempt. The grapevines continued to bear grapes, but now they rotted on the vine.

The pens he built in the backyard behind the garage to house his birds and animals were all empty. The incubator was sold and gone. Even Ole Jim was gone—to one of my uncle's homes, I suppose. That dog just about grieved itself to death without Daddy.

The swing set was still in the yard. But we no longer felt like swinging. There would be no more barbequed turkeys on the grill out back. Visitors were few and far between. Their "main attraction," my dad, was no longer there to welcome them and feed them. The *Tadpol* was sold, along with all the fishing, boating, and hunting equipment.

I would walk through the garage occasionally just to feel my father's presence. There were still pieces of notepaper on his workbench with "to do's." My heart ached when I saw his handwriting.

Yet, the physical reminders were easy compared to the huge, empty emotional spot in our family where a larger-than-life person had been. It turned out that Mother and us girls had been *passengers in Daddy's life*, and enjoying the ride. He was our protector and safety net. Then the ride stopped and we were made to get off. My mother's promise that "nothing will change" had been impossible to keep. Nothing was ever the same again.

Judy, still less than a year old, was a lifesaver in a way. She may well have been the funniest baby I've ever seen or known. She was like a little wind-up doll, able to sing, dance or clown on cue. We would laugh and laugh. Then we would think how Daddy was missing this sweet, funny baby, and then we'd be sad all over again.

Judy was an extremely bright baby and I was quite aware that she, even at that young age, was able to sense that we were sad. She took it upon herself to be the "cheerleader." I worried about what that kind of pressure could do to a little baby. She could probably now write her own book about how it did and does affect her to this day.

Neighbors also proved to be a Godsend. During my mother's despondent years after Daddy's death, our friend and neighbor Mickie Harmon was always there for us. Old Oscar and Miz Harmon had three children. The first two, a boy and a girl, died in their childhood in the 1920s from complications of measles. They later had another daughter, Mickie.

Mickie Harmon was a little older than my mother and was a fixture at our house during the search for Daddy. She had been married once before but had no children. She doted on the three of us girls. She called me "doll baby." She was like a second mother to me.

Mickie was a tall, skinny redhead and one of the most unusual women I had ever seen. Actually, the hair was dyed. It was not a natural-looking red, but something as shocking as Lucille Ball's.

Before she had moved back into her parents' house, she had worked for the government in Tripoli, Libya. She never talked about the work she did there, so who knows what secret things she was involved in. The chances of someone from Cedartown, Georgia, with parents like Old Oscar and Esther Harmon, being able to travel the world in clandestine roles, are as likely as. . . . Well, they're not likely at all.

In her world travels, she had collected all kinds of exotic things, which Miz Harmon had displayed in her modest house. I would walk through each room and marvel at them and wonder about the places where they were made and bought. Mickie instilled in me the desire to travel, and I have lived out that dream in my adulthood.

Mother never argued with Mickie, but just let her pretend we belonged to her. And quite frankly, my mother was in no condition those first few years after my father's death to do much parenting. She was just barely holding herself together.

Mickie bought me my first tube of lipstick, *Young Time Pink*. But in my state of grief after my father's death, no amount of teenage paraphernalia could turn me into the cool teenager like the ones in the Archie comic books, which I had longed to be just a few months before.

If you've ever lived in the South, you learn that sometimes seasons can be skipped. For instance, every five years or so, the winter chill hangs on until mid- or late April. Oh, the flowers and the dogwoods put out and try to bloom, but the chill keeps you from enjoying their beauty up close. Then suddenly, it's 85 or 90 degrees outside. You've skipped spring and gone directly to summer! And that pattern continues without letup through May and June when it becomes hotter than Hades. We say there are two temperatures in Atlanta during the summer: *Hot*. And, *My God, it's hot!*

It would seem that I would "skip a season" of my life—the teenage one. Grief obliterated it. I had moved right into full-blown adulthood.

Old Oscar, Mickie's father, was notified by Uncle Esco of his fears for my father even before he spoke to my mother that November 1957. He knew Oscar would keep an eye on us. And that he did, until we moved out of the house some five years later. He would cut the grass and tend to anything my mother couldn't handle.

Old Oscar also continued to be Oscar. He had a tiny three-room cottage built behind their house for Esther's spinster sister, Dora, when she retired over in Cedartown. He got the bright idea to build an attachment on to the cottage, a three-sided garage. Oscar missed my father terribly, as we all did, but never more than when he began this project. He worked all summer on it, banging that hammer from morning 'til night.

On the day of completion, Miz Harmon invited the whole neighborhood to come for the unveiling, or rather the pulling of the car into the new garage. There were ten or twelve of us assembled. Old Oscar pulls the car into the garage. We waited. And waited. And waited. He never got out of the car.

Finally, he pulls the car out, gets out with a mad look on his face (actually, it was his normal face), then stomps into the house. None of us knew what was going on until Miz Harmon goes in to check on him. Seems he premeasured the building just for the car—not taking into account that it would need to be wider if you actually wanted to open the doors of the car and get out. In spite of our still-empty lives, it was so good to laugh again! And no one would have laughed louder than my dad would if he'd been there to see it.

My mother's grief was so incapacitating that I would hear her cry herself to sleep each night for over a year. She made only one reference to the nature of his death. When her cousin died of cancer within a year of Daddy's death, she said of his widow Colleen, "Colleen had many months to prepare and accept the circumstances. That would be far easier than a sudden death. No time for goodbye. No time for anything. So much harder to accept."

She made it a point to make friends completely outside our former circle of acquaintances. We saw Mama Rich and our father's brothers and sisters infrequently. All this hurt Lynn and me. We had only each other to relate to.

If there was such a thing as "grief counselors" back then, we sure never heard of them. Who could afford such a thing anyhow? Also there's the fact that Southerners are quite proud people, so I don't think we would have reached out.

Mother did, however, seek help for me when I suffered my first migraine shortly after my father's death. I would suffer from them for many years, sometimes more than one per week. I remember how worried she looked when I was sick. I also suffered from depression and anxiety, which would become lifelong conditions. My friends and I joked about me being the only kid in junior high school who had to take tranquilizers.

My mother "moved on," in her own way. She became over-protective of us and, being rather independent souls, oftentimes we would resent her for it. But who could blame her for being worried about losing us? She'd lost so much already.

We moved from our little bungalow when Judy was around five, but she admits she still loves the sound of a back screen door slamming and a train whistle. Both were her memories from our little house in Smyrna. The train track was only two blocks from our house. With no air conditioning, the windows stayed open and you could hear the trains all night long.

Four years after my father's death, Mother married my stepfather, Bob. He was of German descent, born in California and raised in Nebraska. I doubt if he had ever been on a motorcycle. He actually wore suits to work. She might have been able to find someone more different from my own dad, but I doubt it.

My stepfather was very good to us. He started out on a good foot by telling me he knew he could not take the place of my dad, but he would like to be my friend. Many times in his life, he would say that he knew our own father could not love us more than he did. And I believe him. He was a very loving man.

PHYLLIS RICH CARPENTER

We also inherited a stepsister and stepbrother whom we loved from the start. It amazes me that people from completely different families and circumstances can become another united family. It was similar to my dad transplanting a limb from one tree to another in our backyard in Smyrna. Suddenly, a pear grows from an apple tree.

Still, I felt like a duck out of water. It was like being taken off one planet and dropped on to another. And as I watched Judy growing up, she seemed a little like a misplaced child to me, a round peg in a square hole. The right little girl in the wrong life. And there was nothing I could do about it.

From time to time, we would receive sad letters, such as this one from Buford Appleton of Clarksville, Tennessee:

> To the Family of Earl Rich:
>
> I was a friend of Earl's in the Navy on board ship in 1945 and have tried through the Navy to locate him. The last reply that I had I was informed that he was deceased. I was very grieved to learn of this as I had been planning for some time to get together with him and renew our friendship.
>
> If it isn't asking too much, I wonder if some of his family might give me the details. I would sincerely appreciate any information concerning Rich that you might be able to give me.
>
> Yours truly,
> Buford J. Appleton

Of course we sent personal letters to Mr. Appleton, along with news clippings of our father's death. Mother's response to Mr. Appleton was:

> I would be very pleased to have you come by and meet my daughters as I am very proud of them and know that you will be, too, as they have developed into very wholesome, well-adjusted young ladies, which is commendable considering the emotional stress they experienced at an age (9 and 11) when it could have been disastrous to their emotional development.

Thank you for writing. It has meant a lot to the children and me to have an old friend of their dad's interested enough to inquire. I am only sorry you could not have gotten together years ago before Earl died.

One of my mother's cousins from Alabama, Peggy June Elder Thompson, wrote her a sweet letter. Peggy June had been a former Miss Alabama and runner-up in the Miss America Pageant prior to her marriage. She never made the trip to Georgia while my father was missing, having just lost her three-and-a-half-year-old baby boy to leukemia. She wrote:

> People will tell you time will help. But if it does, it really must take a long time. My heartache hasn't lessened any and it has been nearly four months now. The hardest part is to accept and to live with the fact that they are really gone and that it isn't a nightmare you'll awaken from—to find them still here, full of life, happy and oh so lovable.

Years after Daddy's death, I was still *adrift*. I married way too young. I became a mother of four precious children, three sons and a daughter. Finally, I exited out of the very difficult marriage. Both my mother and stepfather died in recent years and I miss them. But being older, I possessed the emotional skills to cope, something I did not have in 1957.

I gave my mother a small gift a few years before her death in 1994. It was a small, charcoal drawing of the Fox Theater, on a tiny easel. Even though she had been happily married to my stepfather for a long time, she got tears in her eyes. I knew exactly why. I don't think I ever gave her anything she loved more.

My greatest struggle through the years has been to hang on to the person I was in 1957. I realized I was a "little girl lost" in June 2003 when Aunt Elaine died at her home in Nashville. Now, in addition to her being the mother of one of my "quadruplet cousins," Sandra, she also is the mother of Priscilla. Priscilla was married to Jerry Reed, the

PHYLLIS RICH CARPENTER

country and western guitar player and star in Burt Reynolds's *Bandit* movies. They had been happily married since they were teenagers.

At the visitation for Aunt Elaine, Priscilla motioned to me to meet some of her and Jerry's friends. She introduced me as "my Uncle Earl's daughter, Phyllis." I nearly cried. I felt as if someone had poured soothing ointment on an open wound. I guess I'd been MIA for a while. Priscilla's remark reminded me of who and what I am. Thank God.

The O'Shields family, too, would have their own struggles. In James' words, "The death of Albert just about killed our parents." The younger children would also say that, "Nothing was ever the same." There was a gloom over their household. None ever heard their parents discuss the tragedy, but couldn't say what they shared behind closed doors.

Neighbors and friends were concerned about Ellen O'Shields in the weeks following Albert's burial. They coaxed her out of the house for a fun night of "bingo" where she won $250. She promptly used the money to pay down the food tab she had run up at the neighborhood market to help feed out of town guests during the search for her son.

She had kept a baby book for each of her seven children. Albert's was a small, paper book entitled, "Our Baby's Record," copyrighted by Pinkham Press, Boston, 1927. In it, she had lovingly handwritten the milestones of her firstborn, Claude Albert O'Shields, born July 12, 1931, in Atlanta, Georgia.

He weighed eight pounds at birth—eighteen pounds by six months. Albert's first word was "here" when his mother asked him to show her where his ball was. The last entry in the small book, recorded by the heart-broken mother was:

> Mr. Earl Rich and Claude Albert went duck hunting and both drowned. Albert died Nov 29-1957. He was drowned. Found on Dec 23-1957 at 10:25 AM. Buried Dec 24-1957 at Westview Cemetery. Albert was 25 years old and he was married to Elaine Bullard on Feb 11-1955.

The ensuing years were not without other difficulties for the family, or the whole world for that matter. My generation's early World War II political vocabulary would now morph into one with a distinctly Southeast Asian flair: Tet Offensive, DMZ, Agent Orange, Ho Chi Minh Trail, Napalm, Viet Cong.

The remaining O'Shields' brothers would be caught up in the middle of the Vietnam "conflict." James O'Shields would receive a wound in Chu Lai, Vietnam in September 1969, which was initially called "non-survivable." He would receive thirty-six pints of blood the first night.

Back at home, a local sheriff would circle the block a number of times looking for the O'Shields' home to notify them of James' plight, as the family watched and worried.

Later James would be sent to a hospital in Japan. His parents were unable to afford the trip to be with him, but brother Robert, who served in Korea and Vietnam, would be detoured to Japan to be with his brother.

James remembers a young wounded soldier in the bed beside him. James and he would make eye contact, and James actually summonsed help from the medical staff for the soldier from time to time. When the soldier's father arrived from the United States, he offered to make a call to James' parents back home in Atlanta.

The father reported to James that his mother's message was, "Fight, fight, fight!" She would keep the five-inch stack of telegrams, which arrived daily from the Army informing her of the progress of her son's recovery. Sadly, the young soldier who had been in the bed beside James died.

Younger brother John would also receive a Purple Heart in Vietnam after his truck was blown out from under him near Pleiku, Vietnam. Finally, youngest brother, Carl, would serve in Vietnam in the same unit as John.

Ironically, Lynn and I would lose a cousin, Donnie, in 1969, the same year that James O'Shields was severely injured. That was the year of the highest casualties, so that the Vietnam Memorial rises distinctly to reflect that statistic. The memorial includes the engraved name of Sgt. Donald Leo Cline.

Donnie Cline was the younger brother and only sibling of Nita Ann Cline, the cousin who had been overcome with grief in our house while my father was missing.

27

My father carried a new gun with him on his last hunting trip, and his grandsons still look for any remains of it to this day. In this modern-day search, I suddenly hear my nephew use the term "Granddad," and I am taken by surprise. My father is frozen in time in my memory as a youthful thirty-five-year-old with young children of his own.

In 2008, I would hear my father referred to as "Granddad" often. It was then that four of Earl Riley Rich's incredible grandsons, hatched a plot to return to the Etowah River to try to find the missing gun and any other personal effects of his. They spent thousands of dollars of their own money for equipment. They risked life and limb.

I'm not sure if it was the *artifacts* they were seeking, or the *connection* to their grandfather. And for reasons perfectly clear to any parent or child, they chose to keep this secret from my sisters and me. The dangers, which are intrinsic to the Etowah, have not subsided with the passage of time.

When I later learned what they were up to, I made the misguided statement that the metal of the guns would be long gone by now, rusted to smithereens. But then, lo and behold, they retrieved a valuable Civil War sword hilt, belonging to a long-dead Union cavalryman. So much for my theory!

A curiosity or longing has formed in our children and they undertake these projects to this day. Nephew Scott, our entrepreneur, had the plan and equipment worked out for the search. My son Craig was the Safety Manager, insisting on ropes and other cautions—which amazes me because he was always my *runs with scissors* kid. My oldest son, Chris, the only redheaded grandson of Daddy, was the scuba diver for deep water pockets. In addition to inheriting his grandfather's love of water and the out-of-doors, he also has his "mechanical genius." He can fix anything, build anything, and locate the problem within any engine or gizmo.

Rounding out the "crew" was nephew Shane, brother of Scott. Scott will tell you his goal was locating the guns. Shane was much more interested in documenting the feat and coming up with answers to the long-standing mystery. He also pointed out to Scott that the original river search area was miles long and they would need to pinpoint where they should start. Scott, one to jump in first and come up with a plan later, had to agree that not knowing where to begin or confine their search *might be a problem.*

So Shane researches for weeks, compiles a report ("Earl Project Facts"), picture-boards and a solid plan. Then the young men must come up with permission from the river landowners. Learning about the circumstances, the owners were very kind and hospitable.

There was much excitement when the sword hilt was found underwater. After digging twenty minutes underwater, Shane pulls up what he first believes to be an old stirrup. After catching his breath, he realizes it's an old sword hilt. An hour later, research on the internet confirmed it was a Model 1860 calvary saber hilt, a Union version.

This is the timeline of the day of hunting spent by his grandfather, Earl Rich and friend, Albert O'Shields, as put together by Shane Oliver:

Earl Project Facts

1) The men were seen "getting in the river" at approximately 8:00 a.m. the morning of November 29 at the Hwy. 61 Bridge near Ladds, just south of Cartersville.

2) The river on the morning of November 29 was "up considerably from recent rains" according to the *Cartersville Tribune.*

3) The water level at Lake Allatoona itself was at 826 feet, a full 14 feet *below* full pool (about average for that time of year).

4) Water had been released every day in the week leading up to November 29, including Thanksgiving Day. More water was actually released Thursday than on Friday when the men drowned.

5) The men floated approximately one mile downstream to an area known as the "Brown Fish Traps" because of its location on the river near Brown Farm. These traps are unique in that they converge at a small (approximately 200-square-foot) egg-shaped island in the middle of the river with a small channel cutting through it. There on the island they set up a blind and began hunting.

6) At approximately 10:30 a.m., a fifteen-year-old boy named Edward Shelton who lived at Brown Farm on the south bank of the river saw the men and called out to them asking if they were having any luck. They replied, "No," and he left. Shelton did not see a boat when he saw the men, but said that it could have been tied at the bank and he could have missed seeing it.

7) According to the Cartersville Tribune, water was released from the dam Friday afternoon "adding to the rising water." The water flow during the release, according to federal records, was approximately 3,831 cubic feet of water per second, which indicates that both of the dam's generators were operating. Tuesday of that week the flow was recorded at 5,314 cubic feet per second, so Friday's release was *typical*, if not slightly *less* than normal. In any case, the water levels downstream would have risen upwards of four feet in a matter of minutes. Records also indicate that *no* water was released from the dam Saturday or Sunday. This confirms reports that Sheriff Atwood had requested that the Corps of Engineers not release water so that the initial searches could be conducted.

8) A passing train crew reported seeing the men at the traps but it is not known at what time they were spotted by the crew. The men were reportedly "in waist deep water holding their guns

PHYLLIS RICH CARPENTER

above their heads." Due to sight-line restrictions from the tracks above, the men would have to be at least 20–25 yards from the bank in order for the engineers to be able to see them.

9) Albert O'Shields' body was found "just below" the traps according to the *Cartersville Tribune.* This would indicate that he was probably dead before he made it 100 yards down river.

Shane concluded his report with these comments:

On a personal note, I have trout-fished numerous rivers in Georgia, including the Chattooga, the War Woman, the Flint River and the Chattahoochee.

In all cases, I have done so wearing shorts with hiking boots in order to give me some semblance of *feel* on the rocks. In some cases, I have spent four to six hours walking downstream over continuous slime covered obstacles.

Walking across rocks in a river is an "art form" of sorts and flowing water approaching even *hip-deep level* poses serious problems. Each and every step requires careful mental assessment of water current pertaining to the particular rocks involved.

You can't just make a beeline across rocks that are submerged. Each particular rock has its own personality and its individual position and angle versus the current (relative to other rocks around it) dictates what course of action you are required to pursue.

Above all else, the ability to see through the water is *imperative.* If you cannot see the rocks that you are trying to step on to, then your forward progress is easily impaired and loss of footing becomes commonplace.

Loss of footing in the case of Earl and Albert (given the conditions in which they were placed at the time) meant certain death. I cannot, under any scenario, imagine the two men traversing the required distance from the island to safety without being swept away by the current that morning.

The *best-case scenario* for me traversing the rock formation of the fish trap was two minutes and fifteen seconds from the south portion of the island.

The same trip from the north portion of the island takes approximately forty seconds more. My attempt was made while wearing polarized glasses to help me see the rocks through the water (which was at its absolute lowest possible level).

Imagine the water level at least three times higher, muddy, rising, with zero underwater visibility and a temperature around 36 degrees Fahrenheit!

The attempt that the two men made to reach shore that day was a lost cause from the start, but a valiant effort nonetheless.

The grandsons' modern-day mission was documented in a Cartersville, Georgia, newspaper:

Unearthed Treasures
The Daily Tribune News
Cartersville, Georgia
March 2, 2010

For Shane Oliver, a search for clues surrounding his grandfather's 1957 drowning has led to an unexpected discovery. At the suggestion of his brother, Scott, he and their cousin, Craig Carpenter, embarked on a journey to find their late relative's shotgun, thought to be underneath the surface of the Etowah River. While the quest continues, their first outing in June 2008 proved to be an eventful one. Along with railroad spikes, fishing lures and a boat anchor, the small diving team discovered the handle of a Civil War sword, which the family recently donated to the Bartow History Museum.

"They had a perfectly good plan," said Shane Oliver, referring to the fateful duck hunting excursion of their grandfather, Earl Rich and his friend, Albert O'Shields. "It would have been a simple hunting trip. When they released the water from the dam that day they didn't have sirens like they do these days. In fact the sirens were put in place because of the drownings. They were just simply on an island duck hunting and the water, after it was released from the dam, made it down to the traps where they were hunting."

"All logic points to the conclusion that they had an aluminum boat with them so if the water starts rising, just hop in the boat. They have a truck parked down the river, [so] just float down there and get in the truck. But for whatever reason a few minutes later they were seen in three feet of water holding their guns above their heads trying to walk across the rocks to make it to shore. To me, the only explanation is they lost their boat somehow when the water started to rise and therefore they had no choice but to try to get to shore."

Never having met his grandfather, Shane Oliver and his close relatives have enjoyed hearing colorful stories about Rich, which paint him as living life to the fullest.

"He was a character," Shane Oliver said. "He was larger than life. If you hear all the stories about him, he was the crazy man who'd be standing up on the seat of a motorcycle with his arms out driving down the middle of the street. To actually see the spot where [the drowning] happened was amazing. . . . The last people to see him alive were engineers on a train passing on the train tracks that actually looked down on the fish traps.

"The engineers were the ones who reported seeing the men in waist-deep water trying to hold their guns above their heads and walk across these fish traps. We've been out there on the fish traps when a train has come by and it's almost like I'm seeing exactly what he saw in the final seconds of his life. I'm on these fish traps [and] there's a thundering train roaring above my head. It's just a really surreal feeling."

After receiving permission from the present landowner near Brown Farm Road in Cartersville, the team started searching with an underwater metal detector. Due to the current, two people held onto Shane Oliver as he dove underwater as potential items were identified.

"The river bottom is [not] mud or silt," said Shane Oliver, who was digging with a small garden hoe. "It's compacted sand and gravel and the hilt was probably 8 to 10 inches under the surface and it took at least 20 minutes of just relentless digging before I could actually get down to it. It was frustrating because it was freezing cold. It was everything I could do not to say, 'Forget it, I've had enough of this.'

"When we finally got to it and I finally cleared it away and pulled it up out of the water, my first reaction was it was an old stirrup. Then it probably took another 30 seconds until we agreed that it was a sword hilt. Had we known what it was I probably would have been digging a little bit more gingerly."

After researching online, the brothers determined the sword handle, also known as a hilt, was a model 1860 cavalry saber that was probably lost in May 1864 when Union troops crossed the Etowah River. They believe it belonged to a soldier in a cavalry unit attached to Gen. John Schofield's 23rd Army Corps.

"We all value history. It's one thing for that sword to be sitting on one of our mantels or coffee tables and it's another thing to put that piece of history back to where people can see it," Scott Oliver said about donating the hilt to the Bartow History Museum. "I think people find things like that and they don't document where they found it and history is lost. So we were able to go back and research and find which army crossed the river there at a spot that was probably unknown to Civil War history books and we kind of wanted to bring that forward—that's why we did this."

While the authenticity of the hilt is intact, the Cartersville museum currently is in the process of collaborating its background story to provide details on its possible owner and his unit's battles. The Civil War relic is one of the latest contributions to the BHM, a venue that relies on the public for its collection of artifacts. Since the museum opened in 1987, it has acquired about 5,000 objects, nearly 11,000 photographs and at least 11,000 documents, most of which have been donated.

"I would say the majority of what the museum owns in its collections were donated from the community of Bartow County and that

PHYLLIS RICH CARPENTER

includes photographs, family papers, business papers and then your objects—household items, quilts, farming implements, business related machines or tools [and] clothing," said BHM Director Trey Gaines. "It's the community that has these items and we're here to collect and preserve them for future generations and part of that is to present it through these exhibits and programs."

Marie Nesmith
Features Editor

Just after this article was published, the Bartow History Museum gave a private tour of the venue prior to opening to the public. Since Daddy's grandsons had donated the hilt to the Museum in honor and memory of their grandfather, my sisters and I, along with children, grandchildren and other family members, would attend this private grand opening.

More than fifty years have passed since the death of my father, but we all still cling to any thread of connection to the wonderful man he was. My niece Holly, her husband, and two sons made the trip from the Chicago area by car, due to Holly's fear of flying. Ironically, Holly is the spitting image of a young Mama Rich. Her two young sons were wide-eyed as we talked about their great-grandfather and made our way around the museum.

We count our children and grandchildren among our many treasures. Each is a daily reminder of our dad and keeps him near to our hearts. Two of our grandchildren have his middle name, Riley.

My sister Judy's son, Spencer, has his claim to his grandfather's genes in his amazing musical ability. A gifted banjo player, as well as other stringed instruments, he has the Rich family's ability to just pick up an instrument and play the heck out of it.

Even Daddy's boat, the *Tadpol*, is still amusing us. My third son, Craig, got his first small boat not too long ago. He called me to tell me he was naming it *Tadpole*, too. But Craig said he wanted to be more serious, to spell his boat's name correctly. When I saw the boat for the first time, he had neatly painted on its side, *Tad Pole*. I laughed so hard

I couldn't even explain to Craig what was so funny. I think he actually surpassed my dad's joke.

My grown son, Corey, visited me from San Diego around the year 2005. I had a business trip in Nashville and he tagged along. Before we left to return to the Atlanta area, we toured the Country Music Hall of Fame.

Now Corey is about as far removed from country music as you can get. But I noticed him hanging around one of the large gold records representing a musician. Then I saw him paying for a CD at the register. I was amazed that he purchased a Johnny Cash CD!

Corey and I drove back home listening to and singing "Jackson." He couldn't have known what that moment meant to me. And when Johnny Cash died, I wrote a tribute to him about how much he had meant to three generations of my family. The *Atlanta Journal-Constitution* published it. Carl O'Shields, whom I would not meet until years later, read the tribute and recognized the name of the daughter of the man who had been killed at the same time as his brother.

Daddy would be proud of all of us. At the same time, he considered himself "ordinary" and would be surprised with all the fuss made over him.

PHYLLIS RICH CARPENTER

28

From that night in the Atlanta funeral home when my mother, sister and I, along with other members of the Rich family visited the grieving O'Shields' family, we had never spoken to or contacted the O'Shields' family again—nor they us. Our singular grief was all we could bear. Then, as I wrote these pages of my father's life and death, I felt an urgent need to reach out to them. After all, this is a story of *two* families.

We learned that Elaine O'Shields died in 2004 of cancer. She had remarried and given birth to a son, Michael Moon, in 1959. I think now about hearing her tell my mom that she was more fortunate—she had my father's children to remember him by.

Elaine would see to it that Michael would be a part of the O'Shields family, even though there was no biological connection. He would say he had three "grannies": Granny Moon, Granny Bullard, and Granny O'Shields. Ellen O'Shields would tell him he was the grandson she never had by her darling Albert. Michael has an unusual connection to Albert O'Shields. His mother showed him the news clippings and told him the story of her first love. He speaks fondly of Albert.

We were then able to phone William O'Shields, Albert's younger brother, who ironically lived less than ten miles from my home. If he was surprised by my call, he hid it well. He agreed at once to a meeting with our family, saying that he was sure his brothers would want to take part. He later admitted to me that he had been looking through the old newspaper clippings about the drownings just days before I called him. He said, "I had always wondered what happened to the two little girls whose picture was in the newspaper."

So it was that on January 4, 2014, my sister Lynn and I, as well as Daddy's grandsons, Shane and Scott Oliver, and several other family members, drove to James O'Shields's home for one of the most surreal events of our lives. We had hoped to speak to at least one of Albert's siblings, but we were blessed to meet all five living brothers. Sister Wilhemina had died twelve years earlier from cancer.

The siblings of Albert and us, the daughters of Earl, are all in our sixties or seventies now. Only Judy was still in her fifties. But on the afternoon of our meeting, we were the children or very young adults we were in 1957—transported back in time in an instant. And feelings of intense grief are never far away. They are merely skin deep.

The O'Shields brothers were happy to see us, but were emotional from time to time. Two brothers, Robert and John, from the very start of our conversation, were visibly saddened to speak of their brother and of the time that he was missing. They didn't need to explain. We knew their pain all too well.

Our visions of Albert all through the years were not entirely accurate. Much of what we had heard was a misconception. We were led to believe that Albert was a much bigger man than our dad, who was 5'11". But as it turns out, Albert was only 5'9."

And then there were the pictures! For the first time, we were able to see the precious images of Albert with his blond, wavy hair and baby face. And he had an uncanny resemblance to my own father. Albert's brothers said he was a friendly sort and it was easy to see that he was the kind of person my dad would want for a friend.

Robert remembers his time at the river search as being freezing cold, stopping only to warm up by the campfires, then jumping back in the boat. He said a number of Albert's friends, including Bobby Johnson, had joined in the search.

Robert looks much younger now than his seventy-nine years. He shared that he still regularly visits the graves of his parents and Albert. On this day of our meeting, he lowers his head in sadness and says, "As a family, we had our ups and downs, but. . ." He is unable to finish his sentence.

PHYLLIS RICH CARPENTER

James, fourth-born son, is smiling, outgoing—a person who probably never meets a stranger. William, third-born brother, asked us all if we had seen the local news about two young men, friends and fishing partners, who were currently missing on Lake Lanier in northeast Georgia. We all nodded yes without comment.

We identified completely with his being drawn to this piece of local news. If you have had a loved one who drowned and was missing at any time, you have a lifelong sympathy for other families in the same situation.

A week after the meeting of the Rich and O'Shields families, the two young men William had mentioned were found dead in the lake. Their families will likely suffer the same fate as us. Absent eyewitnesses, they may never know what happened or how it happened.

The two youngest brothers of Albert, John and Carl, spoke quietly about the sadness of 1957 and how much their oldest brother meant to them.

Our meeting ended with picture taking of Lynn, me, and the brothers. We all concluded that both Earl and Albert were the kind of men who would never have left the river that day without the other. I could see on the faces of these brothers that it is important to them that their brother never be forgotten.

We are two random families plucked from obscurity and bound together forever by the same tragedy. *All because two friends had set out on a fun day of duck hunting.*

Shortly before this meeting, my sisters and I, with the assistance of our sons, had made our own unique journey back to the Etowah River, exactly fifty-five years after our father went missing. Lynn and I would be seeking some reconnection to the bond we once shared with a unique and wonderful father. Judy would be seeking *anything.* It's hard to find something if you don't know what you lost.

The plan was to make the hike to the actual spot on the Etowah where it is believed that the two men died. If this spot was deemed by the 1957 searchers "too treacherous" for us to visit when we were children, you can just imagine how difficult it was when two women in their 60s, another in her 50s and my autistic daughter undertook the trek in 2012! Still, we were determined.

Our sons arranged this trip for us. The property backing up to the Etowah is owned by private individuals—some owning the farms for generations. To obtain permission to go onto the property we needed to access, my son Craig sent an email to a landowner saying, "You have no idea what this will mean to our mothers."

Nephew Scott and his girlfriend met us in Cartersville, along with landowner, Jeremy Knight. My son Craig's ankle injury prevented him from attending. This is not a journey one could make with any kind of injury.

We crossed a flat field on a sod farm, then headed into a thick forest. The forest is typical of Georgia landscape: hilly, treacherous, up and down, vines and fallen trees, along with a rabbit one of us scared out of its wits. Or vice versa.

Lynn and my daughter Cara lagged behind. Judy was so far ahead that at times she was out of my sight. Still the protector, I was trying desperately to keep them all out of harm's way.

My autistic daughter is sometimes unsteady even on flat ground, but she had insisted on coming. When we reached several cliff-like impasses, I advised her to simply slide down muddy cliffs on her rear— to pretend she is evacuating an airplane down a chute. She made the leaps like a pro.

I could hear the water before we reached it. Judy had completely disappeared and I was frantic. When I reached the steep bank, I could see that she had already made the six to eight-foot leap off a cliff to the water's edge below.

PHYLLIS RICH CARPENTER

One of my theories was dashed at the sight of the "drop." I had always imagined that Daddy would toss his gun to the bank when he realized that he was in trouble. Now I could see that the bank was far too high for such a maneuver.

Once I determined that Judy was safe for the moment, I sighed, turn to the landowner, Jeremy, and said, "Well, she is her father's daughter!"

I knew the landowner would be concerned about the liability. But later he would write that the day was a blessing for him, that we had hugged him just like family, and that it made him feel good to see how much love we had for our dad.

Scott was shocked to see the water. He and his brother and cousins had carried out their expedition only at times when water was not being generated from the dam. But this day was a different story. The water was high, raging and covered the little island where Daddy and Albert would have been waiting for the ducks to fly overhead. Only a small tuft of grass was visible.

Scott apologized that we were unable to get closer, but I felt that we were meant to see the site at its treacherous worst. And for us it was a sacred place, no matter what the conditions happened to be.

Nephew Shane had previously described all that we saw and heard that day—the water, the noise, the smell, the bare trees, the grassy island, the whitewater of the rock formations, the railroad tracks—as a "stage" for a tragedy on a Shakespearian scale.

Judy and Lynn had fashioned three small bouquets, each a little different from the other. The plan was for each of us daughters to throw our bouquet into the rushing waters. But I quickly made the decision that Lynn and I would not be jumping down to water level. There was only a small ledge to place your feet upon and we were nowhere near as nimble as we used to be. So Judy tossed each of our bouquets and all three were quickly sucked under the fast-moving water.

To my relief, she finally climbed back up the bank to safety, but not before collecting three small rocks, made round by who-knows-how-many years of being tumbled by the waters of the Etowah. I held mine and wondered if it was in that same spot on November 29, 1957.

On the walk back, I noticed the beauty of the landscape and felt the warm sun on my face. I was amazed that I was smiling. It had not been a sad day after all, but somehow *special*. The years had wiped away the rawness.

I am also older and wiser. I can now look at the one family portrait of the five of us, presented to us the day of my father's funeral, and rejoice. My sixty-plus years of life have taught me that if you have five minutes of happiness, cherish them. Those moments may be rare and short-lived.

No amount of wisdom or age can answer all of life's complex questions. Why do some people pass off this earth and the rest of us let them go with minimal effort? Yet, when others depart, why do we cling to the memory of them and miss them each and every day? I have no answers to those questions and can no longer be bothered with the "why." It's just a fact of life.

My heart no longer breaks for my father, that he died so young and lost everything he valued—*because he had more than most ever will*. He loved being married. He adored my mother and she adored him. He loved being a dad and he doted on us. He thought everything we did was either hilarious or genius, or both. Some men live a hundred years and do not experience the life and love that my dad had in thirty-five years. He is to be envied, not pitied.

My personal saving grace is that I have inherited my father's complete love affair with life itself. I have walked the streets of San Diego, San Francisco, New York City, and Miami and wondered if they look the same as when a young Earl Rich, first time away from home as a sailor in the U.S. Navy, walked them.

PHYLLIS RICH CARPENTER

The human spirit is amazing. It struggles to survive tragedy and to find peace and happiness whenever and wherever it can. I have found both. And they come from knowing who I am.

I am Earl's daughter. And I can close my eyes and become the little girl on the back of a motorcycle, holding on tight to her daddy, flying through the night.

EPILOGUE

My nephew Shane is our family's historian extraordinaire. He put together a timeline of his grandfather's WWII naval service by comparing the Navy's official record of where he was and what he was doing—then cross-checking it with Daddy's letters home from the war. This timeline/epilogue, along with Daddy's letters home, paints a living picture of a very dark time in history. And it contains some really cool website links that practically transform us back in time!

Military service timeline for:
<u>Earl R. Rich</u>
<u>Ser. No. 269-13-89</u>

2/24/42	Enlisted in Macon, GA (Apprentice Seaman)
2/25/42 – 4/14/42	Basic Training in Norfolk, VA
4/16/42 – 5/1/42	Advanced Training in Norfolk, VA
5/4/42 – 6/6/42	Submarine Chaser Training in Miami, FL
6/8/42 – 7/14/42	New York, NY while PC-489 is readied for service – S2c Guarded the damaged SS *Normandie* for two weeks <u>www.youtube.com/ watch?v=XdCXDkFOLfA</u> April 22nd partied at the *Stage Door Canteen* in NY with actress Hope White June 20 met Jack Dempsey at his restaurant (Broadway & 42nd St.)
7/14/42 – 10/13/43	PC-489 South Atlantic and Caribbean (based in Recife, Brazil) Escorted ships from Trinidad/Recife/Bahia. Once sailed up Amazon for repairs. Earl was a gunner's mate manning the port side 20 mm Oerilkon Cannon

www.youtube.com/watch?v=6oFNWPJGyXc

7/14/42 PC-489 is commissioned and sets sail. Earl's tonsils go bad. Mid July 42 – Hospitalized in New London, Conn with Tonsillitis

8/1/42 Brooklyn, NY still recovering from Tonsillitis

9/1/42 Depth charge attack on German sub per Earl. Attack unsuccessful.

9/5/42 Dry-docked in Miami for repairs (maybe from the attack on the sub)

9/42 Guantanamo Bay, Cuba

12/42 South Atlantic Fleet sent to Recife, Brazil. Earl gets a letter from someone named Patricia Reed.

1/1/43 GM3c

1/31/43 Crossed equator. (PC-489 actually crossed the equator 50+ times)

2/5/43 Back to home base in Recife, Brazil. Earl's friend, Calvin Athy, drowns.

2/15/43 Another unsuccessful attack on German U-Boat.

4/43 Ten days leave to visit home

7/11/43 GM2c

8/13/43 Volunteered for a "ride along" on a submarine and looked through the periscope. Earl clearly wanted to be on a sub but his parents objected.

10/5/43 Recife, Brazil after his last convoy escort aboard PC-489

10/14/43 – 11/6/43   Home

PHYLLIS RICH CARPENTER

11/7/43 – 11/22/43	Washington D.C. for more training – Gunner's Mates School
11/23/43 – 12/11/43	Cross country to San Pedro, CA
11/24/43	Memphis, TN
11/26/43	Juarez, Mexico and El Paso, TX
11/27/43	Phoenix, AZ
12/11/43	San Pedro, CA
12/12/43 – 12/24/44	USS Giraffe – GM1c – In charge of all gunner's mates on board and getting all the ship's guns in working order.
	2/2/44 Crossed equator
	2/7/44 Crossed 180th Meridian
	2/10/44 Funafuti Atoll, Ellice Islands
	6/44 – 7/44 Eniwetok Atoll
	7/17/44, 10/4/44, 10/6/44 Marshall Islands
	8/7/44 – 8/10/44 Assault on Saipan
	9/20/44 Guam
	11/44 Ulithi Atoll
	10/14/44 Caroline Islands
	12/44 Palau, Caroline Islands (Peleliu)
12/25/44 – 1/22/45	Home
1/23/45 – 6/5/45	Washington D.C. – Training Gunner's Mates & Electric Hydraulics. Patricia Reed came up to New York and stayed with him during this time
6/16/45 – 7/12/45	Training and Distribution Center in Shoemaker, CA. Waiting to be assigned to a new ship
8/6/45 – 8/18/45	ComServ 7th Fleet Navy 3149 (Samar Island, Philippine Islands). He arrived in the Philippines the day the atomic bomb was dropped.
8/24/45	AATC Navy 3002 (Subic Bay, Luzon, Philippine Islands)

9/2/45	Japan officially surrenders and the war is over.
11/20/46	Officially discharged from the Navy.
	Received ribbons:
	Asiatic Pacific
	Good Conduct
	American Theatre
	Philippines Liberation
	World War II
	Victory

PHYLLIS RICH CARPENTER

REFERENCES

Body that Drowns (redOrbit.com), by Gary Haupt, Feb. 2006.

The Earl Facts, Earl Report, Naval Timeline, by Shane Oliver.

A River Runs Through It and Other Stories, by Norman Maclean. Reprinted by permission of the University of Chicago Press.

Old Folks—Our O'Shields & Knowles Families, by C. Allen O'Shields, copyright 2013, allen@allenoshields.com

PC - Patrol Craft of World War II – A History of the Ships and Their Crews, by William J. Veigele, Ph.D., USNR (Ret). Astral Publishing Co., astralpublishing.com.

Edwards Brothers Malloy
Thorofare, NJ USA
August 28, 2014